SISTER

HEALING IN COMMUNITY

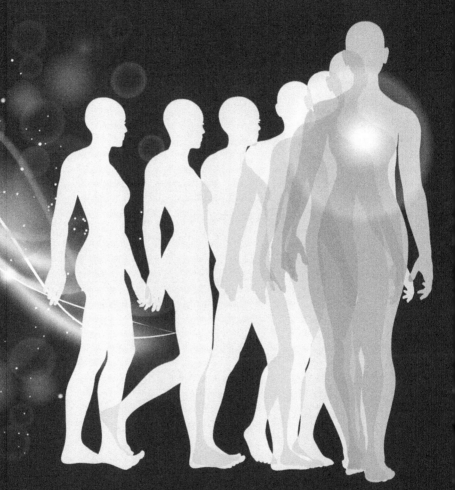

TIFFANY MARIE BOERNER

FEATURING: Kimichelle Bain, Jen Bates, Mary Blanchard, Jill Ann Brooks, sekayi anika, Jenny Campanilla, Bonnie Casamassima, Jennifer Chavez, Megan Crouch, Kate Day Roosma, Vila Donovan, Ashley Hoobler, Nicole Jackson, Thais Krause, Mary Lloyd, Ellen Mathys, Kelbi McCumber Morris, Jordan O'Connor Ana Palla, Janice Pouch, Bruja Carrie Liz Ramos, Wendie Veloz, Hayley Verney, Sheri Welsh

DEDICATION

This book is dedicated to the Armor of Light, to the supportive realms of Spirit, angels, master teachers, and departed loved ones for their unwavering love and guidance. To the Divine infinite intelligence for channeling through us that which others need to hear.

To fellow light-workers, healers, and mediums of integrity: thank you for standing tall and courageous in truth. Together may we remain committed to our contribution to the planet.

In honor of the sage authors of Sister Armor, thank you for answering the call to connect to your medicine with the intention of lifting and healing. To your beautiful hearts that want to heal and create a positive contribution to our planet. Each of us is a symbol of loyalty, strength, courage, and devotion to the highest love. As we prevail together, we remember, we (re) connect, we know our truth, and heal.

Sister Armor

Healing in Community

Tiffany Marie Boerner

Copyright © 2022 Tiffany Marie Boerner

Published by Brave Healer Productions

Print ISBN: 978-1-954047-59-4

eBook ISBN: 978-1-954047-58-7

DISCLAIMER

This book offers words of wisdom regarding physical, mental, emotional, and spiritual wellbeing and is designed for educational purposes only. You should not rely on this information as a substitute for, nor does it replace professional medical or business advice, diagnosis, or treatment. If you have concerns or questions about your health, business, or mental wellbeing, you should always consult with a physician, other healthcare professional, or business professional. Do not disregard, avoid or delay obtaining medical or business-related advice from your healthcare or business professional because of something you may have read here. The use of any information provided in this book is solely at your own risk.

Developments in research may impact the health, business, and life advice that appears here. No assurances can be given that the information contained in this book will always include the most relevant findings or developments with respect to the particular material.

Having said all that, know that the women here have shared their tools, practices, and knowledge with you with a sincere and generous intent to assist you on your journey to wellness. Please contact them with any questions you may have about the techniques or information they have provided. They will be happy to assist you further!

TABLE OF CONTENTS

A MESSAGE
TO THE READER

My mom and I were cleaning her kitchen one day. She had emptied the contents of every cabinet from every shelf available to her—piles of dishes, Tupperware, and small kitchen appliances stacked on the kitchen table and chairs. As I scanned the mess, I felt overwhelmed, and really, I wanted no part of this deep cleaning. "Mom, I thought we were cleaning the kitchen. Not making a complete mess of it." Scrubbing a shelf with her soapy rag, "You have to make a mess before you can clean." I was maybe 17 years old at the time. Today, I *see* the messes I've had to make in order to clean. The messy relationships, awful jobs, and attempts to succeed, but felt I'd failed. All of it has to be messy before it can be clean. Life is raw and usually messy, and the process of cleaning is sacred.

As authors, we experienced personal transformation as we brought in the material for this book. Connecting with aspects of ourselves in this reflective way further aligns us with the true beauty of an unlimited self. We're forever evolving, shifting, and morphing deeper and deeper into our truth. This has granted each of us great healing. For this, we're grateful.

There is deep healing when we share our stories. We're witnessed. The story itself becomes armor that holds us up, sustains us, and allows us to organize the magnitude of our experience into meaning. When we share our truths that contain fear, struggle, and sadness and have our truth received and validated by other women, we heal. We're allowing one another to see and hear one another. In this, we find the importance of also needing to hear other women's stories in order to see and embrace our own.

Another woman's story becomes a mirror reflecting a self in a way we haven't allowed ourselves to be seen before. Her questions may raise your own. Her conflicts may illuminate your own. Her resolutions invite your own hope. Her strengths aid in your remembering of your own. The Divine feminine is rising. She brings with her force of creation. Expanding and awakening all along her path. May you welcome her rise within you. You are wild—a brilliant force of nature. When it's right, if you haven't already, you'll find yourself surrendering to the blissful opening.

The energies held within this book are transformational and timely. Spiritually, we have relied upon institutions and organizations, and even our own minds to give us the sense of power and connection we've desired. The day of waiting for someone stronger, better, and smarter to come along and figure things out is over. Only us, our very will and remembrance, that leads us to experience the innate spiritual power we can use in our everyday lives. Knowledge is essential, yet without the heart's guidance, it's incomplete.

Our hope is that you see yourself in these shared stories. As you read her story, notice how it may quicken and clarify your own. Open yourself and receive the healing light-filled intentions. May these stories unfold and reveal the unknowns before you. Let them teach you, lift you, and guide you. Remember, you are light, and your humanness is absolute perfection. As you navigate your healing you'll find like-minded communities. Synchronicities will intertwine throughout your days. Be in gratitude and rest. See life's events and exchanges as lessons to learn and expand. Use discernment. Learn the language your body speaks and honor it. She is organized and highly intellectual.

We are here to unravel from attachments of fear, shame, and lack. We're here to break barriers, binds, and untruths. We dispel and dissolve such bonds, ties, and jails. We're free from all that does not align with our highest good. What does not reflect our heart's truth, may it be lovingly lifted, transmuted, and transformed.

Energy is infinite. It's not contained. Energy does not have barriers or structures. Just like you, it's ever-flowing and abundant. As it moves through us, it aligns with our frequency, forming a unique language special just to us. As you honor your unique relationship with energy, enjoy it. Play, grow, and explore with pure wonder. Let go of judgment and trust this innate relationship. Do not box yourself in. Never allow anyone to box you in and dictate your light connection, conviction, and truth. How you weave and dance with medicine is your unique thumbprint, and it's to be honored and protected.

As we move through such evolutionary shifts in consciousness, we'll find ourselves releasing from relationships, jobs, and what we've called home. New relationships will present themselves that'll catapult us into higher versions of self. Life will continue to bring people who reflect all of who we are as if they knew where to find the hidden aspect of us that we never allowed others to see. We encourage you to be all of who you are. Let these stories make you want to be all of you for the world to see! If you find yourself no longer resonating with particular relationships, trust what's occurring. Trust what you're feeling.

And so, dearest sister, a heart of gratitude to you for allowing yourself to step fully and completely onto your path along with so many others committed to walking in the light of truth, peace, and love. May we stand together, moving together in our ordinary lives with an extraordinary perspective. You are a point of light within an amazing, infinite light that permeates all of life and every soul in the Universe. We want you to know that you hold a light that only YOU can shine. We believe your light is unique and vital to the illumination of humanity. Together, our lights will shine and will brighten the path for all who choose to join. You'll know when the time is right for you. When that moment arrives, you'll set your feet upon the path. We can't trivialize the moment we touch the hem of the Spirit world. And together, we will do what we could never do alone.

My high love to you,
Tiffany Marie

A MESSAGE FROM SPIRIT

What a glorious time to connect in harmony and partnership of all things.
In the depths of darkness is your light.
In the weight of darkness is your strength.
In the will of truth is your expansion.
In the wake of loss is realization.
May there be plenty before you.
May the gifts be abundant before you.
A grandeur of Light you are. An expansion of curiosity and wonder of delight.
Thank you for the gifts you share and that you give forth. In love and gratitude.

FOREWORD

By Katya Lidsky, Writer and Dog Relationship Coach

When we think of armor we think of what? Steel. Sword. Shield. Maybe we think of covers and bombs, of protection and metal. But what if some of the biggest work we have to do in this life is to look at armor differently, to redefine what is strong? What if the armor we need most is connection, is intuition, is healing? What if bearing our weaknesses and our struggles, our pain, and our yearnings is the most generous thing we can give and receive?

These are the questions answered within these pages, not through prescriptions and indignant finger-wags, but through abundant sharing and honest acts of service. This is a book about journeys and surviving, not because it was easy but precisely because it was hard. Women, the feminine, the circle of the feminine, is the most resilient force, and it is the core of the gift you're holding in your hands. It was made by you, for you, because of you. Because when one woman supports another, heals another, helps another, there is a ripple effect of goodness and power that can be felt in bones, in dirt, in the vibrations that—right this very minute—bond you to me and me to you through these words. This is where Sister Armor started from, the birth of a movement, a need to tell you how much you mean.

For me, healing and holding always comes back to animals, loving them, being loved by them, and knowing I have access to a power greater than me each time I commune with an animal. It focuses how I eat, how I live, what I believe, who I am. To save animals, to advocate on their behalf feels like the most feminine work in the world because every system that benefits off the backs of animals rides on the mother. On the female. On more. And so you see, my tenderness for this book exists because that feminine circle is wide; it knows no bounds of class, race, status, even species. We are in it together. We must be. To embody the radical act of removing the shell is to embrace defenselessness, our own and others. There is nothing more ferocious to me than loving a defenseless animal. There is nothing more stunning, no blessing more holy, than letting an animal who needs you into your heart and home.

It's intimidating to reveal so much to you. It's intimidating to write about such big ideas, like friendship, wisdom, and rising up. It's intimidating to write amongst brilliant authors with their integrity and their hearts wide open to be viewed, to be taken, to be held, to be stretched infinitely, so there is more space for you. But when I sit down to write, I think not about myself or my ego, but instead about how many of these writers shifted and discovered how they found and heard themselves, and then everything trapped up in a tangle of my worries fades away until all that is left is what matters. The truth matters, and you'll find it here. Trusting matters, and it will be offered to you. Surrender matters, taking the armor off to find that you are fierce and soft, durable and flexible, beautifully weeping and hurting and fighting and yielding. You are everything. You have everything inside of you. Light bounces off of you because you are made of light. Armor off, authentic you, and you are enough.

The women writing in this book and what they share are proof of that because they are just like you, and that is why you are drawn to them. You will feel it; you will dance to the heartbeat of this book and realize just how much you belong. As the teachers and community leaders and facilitators and healers across these pages speak to your soul, I hope you believe in whatever it is you dream of because I believe that the ability to enjoy is a choice. Nothing less. Nothing more. And you deserve to enjoy.

So choose with this circle. Manifest with this circle. Accept with this circle. Let go with this circle. Pinpoint your ease and your flow and go along for the ride and sing in the face of alignment, and splash in the warmth of the ocean underneath the moonlight. For that is what this is. It is fullness and depth; it is real and grounded, but also divine. While you read about these great unravellings, about liberating the self from unhealthy systems and habits, about fleeing societal pressures for freedom, I encourage you to shout into the night. While you get wrapped up in developing new belief patterns or learning how to better the health of your mindbodyspirit, I encourage you to laugh whether you're alone or in public because the space that runs through every writer you are about to fall in love with also runs through me, and it runs through you, and it runs through everyone, and all it takes is one laugh to sync up.

I believe in alternative modalities to healing, recovery, and peace. I believe that what we believe defines us because it creates the evidence we seek. But beliefs are not permanent, and everybody needs literature to remind them of that fact. Everyone needs guides to provide new ways of thinking and a safe place to take a breath. I'd like to think of *Sister Armor* as that, your breath spot. Mess up, try again, face challenges with a smile, with a curl of your lip, with a roar, with vulnerability, with all of it, messy and rich and complex, because you are breathing, here, now, with these women who have been waiting for you.

These women want you to know that you can change your life. There are people gifted enough to support you in doing so, and there is no way of knowing what approach—or when an approach—might work for you. So all we can do is live and learn, witness others who live and learn, and find our circle. Reassess, re-identify, relax, restore, readjust, reaffirm, reach, rebel, and reap. Sometimes I need to read something in black and white for it to hit me and for me to absorb it. Sometimes I need to sit with women armored with their genuine love to know I'm home.

Whether you like a chapter or a tale, a person or a tone, everything you will read is pure, sincere, and offered to you with no obligations but with one request: that you love yourself a little more than you did before you picked up this book and do what is necessary or required in order to nurture that love, take care of it, cherish it, and grow it. This is about that; this is for your wellbeing, you wonderful woman who is awake and ready. The experts you will hear from are educated, experienced, gentle, and game-changing, and they wish to whisper in your ear, to listen to your heart, and to stand by your side. With their fortitude, you can take off the earthly traps put upon you, strip away the expectations and the heavy judgments, and release yourself to the sharp, bright power that is you, that wants to be you. Open to receiving and soaring and passing on what it feels like to drop into your most unguarded state, the armor-less armor where you can be raw, where your weapon is your compassion, and your touchpoint to the solutions you're looking for or the life you seek is simply sisterhood. Link your arm in ours and watch as a chain morphs into an infinity loop.

Come in, come in. We're all animals. Nature is ours. Mother Earth is everywhere; she is us, she is you, and she never leaves you. Neither do books. Join the family.

CHAPTER 1

UNRAVEL

THE STORY OF SISTER ARMOR

Tiffany Marie Boerner, The ReConnective Way Creator,
Divine Light Channel, and Evidential Medium

My sister-friend sent me a beautiful cardigan. It hung down at my knees; the delicate tassels tickled the back of my calves. It wrapped around my body just as the wings of an angel would. The yarn was thick, and the weaving was thoughtfully stitched. Each thread was individual, yet there was no denying the intricate weave making it complete. She and I would joke about how we were cut from the same cloth. Completely the same, yet so different. Plenty of times, we've stirred things up and pounded the drums together until the magic rose. We'd dance and play, cause a ruckus, and lead in shenanigans. Many times, throughout many lives, we've given and received from one another. There is no denying the rhythmic heartbeat of our cyclical soul relationship. In many instances, we've provided armor for one another. On this day, a rather simple cardigan became a spark, the catalyst for great movement: Sister Armor.

It was a Friday morning; I stood in front of my closet coordinating my new cardigan with the perfect pants and top. My sister-friend's loving gesture helped me feel confident and celebrated. I mean, it is *just* a cardigan. But on that particular day, it was far more than that.

I arrived early to work, filled my coffee cup, and settled at my desk. Out of the corner of my eye, I noticed one of my seniors oddly walk past my office door. I could tell he was up to something. However, when he passed my door for a second time, I had an all-knowing sense wash over me. *I was his focus. MMM.*

I took a couple of deep breaths and literally sat still for several minutes, sipping my hot coffee. I savored the quiet mornings in the building. I would go in extra early just to work in the quiet. I'd keep my office lights off until the building would fill with colleagues. The harsh lights would stimulate my nervous system and make me buzz, so I kept them off as long as I could.

Through the threshold of my office door entered a colleague from human resources and a top senior. *I knew it.* I had just signed a contract for the new year and received raving reviews of my commitment, dedication, and achievements. Yet, having had these two individuals enter my office in this fashion, the message was clear. I was being fired.

HR read the script directly at me. I was calm and present. We sat at a large meeting table centered in the office, the lights still off, HR sat to my right and my top senior directly in front of me. Sharply, the script was spoken, yet I was most amused by how my boss had to work at *not* making eye contact with me. Chin to chest and head hung low. *How cowardly,* I thought. I continued to stare across the table; I had nothing to hide. When people show you who they are, believe them. I signed my release papers then proceeded to gather my items. In that very instant, I felt untethered. I worked in this very space for ten years. *What was actually mine to collect?* Everything and nothing. I had a thoughtful exchange and intention for every item in that office. My office was built with the intention to be a safe container, and it served many of us in subtle loving ways.

"Never bend your head. Always hold it high. Look the world straight in the eye." -Helen Keller

I repeated this quote in my heart as I walked down the corridor.

I took the weekend to integrate my new reality. There were moments I succumbed to overwhelming feelings of unworthiness, locked down in fear of what was to come. *What now?* I stared out the window a lot that weekend. I was either filled with rushing thoughts and exaggerated emotions, or I was completely empty, simply existing. The Universe certainly has its way of pulling us from one path while clearing new paths before us. *Why am I here?* I contemplated. *What am I to take away from this? Help me recognize the gift in this clearing. Help me to see and follow the path cleared before me.*

I looked to identify the connection to honor and understand it, so I could release it and let go. At this point in my life, I was carrying significant unhealed trauma and debilitating insecurities and was successfully hiding from living my fullest. I'm worthy of great things. I knew this, but I didn't *know* this.

I was presented with the greatest leap of my life. My path changed for the better, yet it required trust. I had to trust myself. My inner source is sage, and I now needed to learn to listen inward. I was unraveling.

Looking back, this had been coming for some time. Weeks before being fired, I cried driving to work. Just several months prior, at lunch with a dear friend, I announced, "I am done! This will be my final year here." Both of us were caught off guard. *That came out of nowhere,* I thought. Something was brewing within me.

I surrendered to the rock bottom of the complete unknown. In stillness, I found footing in the depths of my will. And, soon enough, I felt deep liberation by knowing that I am more than a job or any label for that matter. Change actually felt possible. I was open to the greatest change. Strength doesn't come from what you can do, it comes from overcoming the things you thought you couldn't do. I released my grip. *I can't live in survival mode anymore. This way of being is depleting my vitality and Spirit.* I stopped living in structures that kept me spoon-fed by external forces. I outwardly forgave myself for failing to dream bigger, for not trusting, for not using my voice, and for not allowing my intellect to be recognized. None of these façades belonged to me, but I held onto them all as if they did.

I rested. I deeply rested, and for weeks, I cried, celebrated, played, and slept. I'd sit in the grass and slowly breathe, watching the autumn leaves gracefully fall around me. If mother earth can let go, so can I. This was a time of grieving and gratitude.

My husband held me so brilliantly through all of the messiness. Wholeness isn't being without sadness or fear; wholeness is all of this. It was accepting myself that allowed me to heal. We were in our bedroom, putting laundry away in silence. "I'm changing. I see myself doing things differently. I'm exhausted. I feel like I am back to crawling." I haven't had the energy to recognize how he's directly affected by my actions. "Are you okay?" I ask him. "Do you want to talk? How are you feeling?" He gave a gentle smile and said, "Tiffany, you just keep getting better."

For the first time in months, I was able to take a deep breath. I stopped apologizing and started saying thank you. Sometimes between acts of great courage, we need space. My husband knew just how to offer that necessary space. I was able to acknowledge and nurture this seedling of knowledge, which brought me to light-filled paths and purpose! And, just like that, I made a decision that would end up being the best one I'd ever make. I took the leap. I set out to open my own business.

I gave myself to the creation of my new business. I achieved my nutrition coach certification, dedicated myself to advancing in personal training, and soon opened the doors to Sister Armor Wellness. Sister Armor Wellness was created to support women in awakening their innate power through nutrition and fitness. For two years, I had the opportunity to serve nearly one hundred women. This felt invigorating and confirming. I was proud of my clients and myself. We had accomplished a lot together!

Though, as time went on, I noticed weekly check-ins morphed into intuitive guidance sessions. As my clients spoke to their ebb and flow, I received guided messages from Spirit. I offered these guided messages but never shared that their guides were the actual voice of graceful guidance.

It is fear that consumes the heart. Support her in alleviating such untruths. Guide her to open the heart, so she may receive. The healing is in acceptance.

My body would fill with Divine love for them. My ego lifted as Spirit-filled me. There was no judgment toward them or myself. I began seeing the blocks behind their struggles. Their loved ones in Spirit form would reveal trauma in ancestral lines. An ancient wise grandmother once appeared very clearly.

You are celebrated for your courage. We lift you and shield you from densities. Your healing is our healing. You, a part of a great collective of souls who helps nurture one another throughout lifetimes. We thank you.

Ascended Masters would present themselves, as would the Angelic realm. Master Teachers would pour through the energetic lines revealing areas of healing.

As time passed, nutrition and fitness plans felt meaningless. I felt my work was perpetuating their disassociation. This didn't completely resonate; something was amiss. My intent was to guide them to a higher place of self-realization and radical self-love. I don't believe women need directions on how to honor their organic body. We simply need to remember. Women are well equipped with powerful senses that guide our every need—an instinctive line of communication between our heart and body that supports us endlessly. Whether we consciously connect with it or not, our body will keep us alive. Whether we embrace it or are in judgment, the body will remain the bridge to the infinite. Our heart holds an ancient love language. Once recognized and connected, we don't need external directions. We're programmed to disconnect from our innate medicine. As natural caretakers, we've forgotten how to intuitively care for ourselves. At times, it can feel near impossible to listen. Rest. Generation after generation is distracted and manipulated by external noise, directed by *"shoulds"* that suspend and deplete our intuitive creativity. Our inherent needs are not meant to be tended to in stolen moments.

My earliest memory of channeling was around age four. I vividly remember a different sensation flowing through my body. I also remember not feeling alone - never without a sense of love or comfort. I had an awareness of a never-ending presence. I was nine years old when I realized I was communicating with something I couldn't physically touch or see yet could feel and see. I never felt threatened. It was quite the opposite—a very different feeling from that of the boogie-man. As an only child, I'd stay with the adults regardless of the event. From pre-teen through my late teens, channeled messages flowed through me at various gatherings. I outwardly shared them. In return, the responses typically included silence or a side-eye, with an apathetic comment of some sort. "Wow, smart kid." And they'd continue in their ordinary conversation. By age 20, I asked "it" to stop—the messages, the sensations of love and comfort, all of it. Begrudgingly, *I don't want you.*

I began meditating every day, an endearing time of sitting with Spirit. The love experienced with Spirit transforms the heart. What I experienced with my clients was just the tip of the iceberg. I knew there was so much to understand and explore. One morning, I entered my meditation with the intention of subtle energy healing.

What is healing outside of the physical body? Please show me how I can help alleviate trauma in those who actively seek healing.

Spirit walked me to an apple tree. Together we stood, the branches arched over us, forming a canopy of leaves and ruby apples. Spirit pointed to an apple and said, "Your focus is here, redirect it there." "There," was the roots of the tree. *The healing is in the roots.* Not at a surface level. *Ah! But of course, thank you, Spirit.*

Layer by layer, within each dimension, a rich opportunity to heal presents itself. The intricacies of our highly organized intelligence are free to us. Being human is a glorious voyage, an expansive privilege, indeed. It's our curious hearts that lead us to revel in remembrance, faithfully falling in love with all that we are. I AM. A valiant dive into the ocean, I swim against the current, rise above the crust, and catch the wave. I AM here for this, a harmonious orchestration available, fully supported by Divine realms so long as I'm willing to make the valiant dive.

Every day I sat in stillness with wide-eyed wonder and a commitment to seek, heal, learn, and understand, establishing a sacred relationship with light consciousness. I opened my heart to my Divine Self that I'd ignored and pushed away. I felt a deeper connection. I never called upon healing from Spirit before, but I began. I began inviting this connection. The sincere connection I cut off many years ago was patiently and unconditionally there for me. Nothing is wasted. Not time. Not love. Not experiences. It all has purpose.

I took baby steps which allowed me to ease into new practices. I began holding space for what we affectionately call 'the little things in life.' I sat with plants to connect with them. I took turns holding different crystals to sense their unique energy: trial and error. I began documenting how I was sensing messages. I became a student of subtle energy. I was learning how to apply intuitive tools that came naturally. I learned how everything around me has an energy field and how it communicates with me and how I receive those communications. I could not stop tuning in to listen. Being outdoors was soon a different experience. I could sense Mother Earth's pulse: Trees hummed, songbirds had a different frequency, the healing force of water, the chatty flowers in my garden.

Everything everywhere was suddenly turned up, and I couldn't *not* hear it. I recognized and experienced pure love, the miracle of life all around

↳ My heart almost yelled — "to Love and BeLoved!"
I thought, Daniel, Yes. As a Man,
Then noticed Binx sitting apart who had just been

me, just as it had always been, but I was finally tuned in. My study soon went further, and I began taking courses to help establish confidence in using my intuition. I started with muscle testing, then Reiki, mediumship development, and shamanic practices re-connecting to what lived within me, awakening my sage soul who lived a thousand lives collecting wisdom and will, grace and endurance.

My awakening showed me a life of devotion. I'm devoted to connecting with Mother Earth and her medicine, healthy eating, embodiment, and healing. I devote myself to intuitive creativity, self-regulating, solitary hiking trips, and ritual. I devote myself to sensing the truths of our interconnectedness, the infinite energy. The greatest intellect resides in this devotion. My work is to sit still and sense the unlimited possibilities in this life, not to operate under step-by-step directions through a filter provided by another.

Without a doubt, my work with Sister Armor Wellness expanded by incorporating intuitively-led practices and exercises. Clients took interest in one on one intuitive sessions and energy healing. The option for alternative healing was a viable line of support for their overall health and vitality. Clients left sessions in a state of peace and calm, commenting that it was easier to tackle ordinary to-dos that otherwise caused them stress. They were practicing discernment and setting boundaries. They found their footing, retreating to nature and cherishing heart connections. Creative play didn't have to wait for stolen moments! They discovered the meaning and purpose of their relationships, including the most important relationship—the relationship with their heart and body. They were able to witness how all they needed was accessible within. Alongside Spirit, my job was to lovingly encourage their journey toward deep self-discovery with unconditional self-love, illuminating the path before them.

I continued to participate in workshops, courses, and development gatherings. I met others who were on a parallel path. All of whom significantly impacted my spiritual expansion. There was so much to understand. The lessons they provided gifted me a new depth of clarity. Not only was I learning how I use my innate intuitive tools, but how others innately use theirs! Some of my greatest lessons took place directly by experiencing shadow. This work led me to a greater realization of my light. There were certainly obstacles, but none insurmountable. I stood in my conviction. My

OH! Heart!

giving me her most ~~outrageous~~ cour- love! OH! I am stunned experience with the Divine gave credence to my purpose. All of it brought wholeness to my heart, unwavering from my truth.

Sister Armor Wellness dissolved as I stepped into subtle energy healing full-time. January of 2018, I became the proud founder and owner of Body & Soul Connection. However, the mission and heart of Sister Armor never ceased. It's with a heart of gratitude as I sit here today and share this with you: I can say with absolute certainty that I AM increasingly aware of my innate goodness and my innate God-ness. Some days, I have to remind myself there's nothing wrong with me. There are patterns to unravel from, new behaviors to embody, and wounds to heal. I'm unlearning generations of pain and remembering love. At this moment and in all moments, I'm completely loving and whole, my soul, an exquisite love story, and I remember. My journey, while tumultuous at times, has been graced with an equal measure of indefinable richness.

The heart is a direct gateway to greater divine intelligence, and when we live in harmony with it, we live in harmony with the wholeness of life. How grateful I am to be alive in this moment with you. How beautiful we truly are. I continue to fall in love with the oneness that we are. Thank you for the heart-led, courageous creations you birth into this world every day and in every way. It matters; it all matters. Unravel only to realize you already are everything you need. Trust in your will and break free. We are meant to live in our highest potential; let's not be imposed by the stories placed upon us and spoken into us. We are worthy of that much, my dear.

Tiffany Marie is the owner of Body & Soul Connection. She is the Creator of ReConnective Way Healing Program, an evidential medium, and a Divine Light Channel. Tiffany's soul mission is rooted in global healing. Her purpose is to support others in ReConnecting what was separated from the human energy field, resulting in abundant spiritual and vital health. Tiffany is a certified Reiki teacher, ancient medicine timeline healer, sound healing and breathwork facilitator, and Integrated Energy Therapy. All acted as an unlocking for her purpose-led and heart-filled work. Tiffany's most recent focus is working with Spirit to spread The ReConnective Way Healing Program beyond her immediate community.

Tiffany Marie is also an author, public speaker, and is active hosting sacred circles that harness intuitive abilities for infinite self-love and wholeness. She's a life-long student who loves to write, think outside of the box, and connect to Mother Earth through plant life and the animal kingdom. Tiffany is a sage light-channel dedicated to transcribing forgotten ancient healing scripture. She holds a strong passion for guiding others through their personal journey of self-discovery. With extensive study, classwork, and community shares, Tiffany Marie continues to deepen her understanding of the foundation of energy healing and the possibilities of emotional and physical healing. With a heart of being of service, she connects with Divine Source consciousness to guide her work. Her personal story continues to motivate others to reclaim their Divine power. Tiffany Marie is committed to the ongoing work of The ReConnective Way Healing Program. Keep an eye out for her and opportunities to receive and become a part of The ReConnective Way Healing Program. Otherwise, you can find Tiffany Marie barefoot playing in nature and being with her family.

Connect, receive healing, teachings, or schedule a sacred circle with Tiffany Marie

Website: www.bodyandsoulconnection.com
Instagram: www.instagram.com/bodysoulconnection
Email: bodyconnectsoul@gmail.com

CHAPTER 2

A RECOVERING PERFECTIONIST'S JOURNEY TO HEALING

Kate Day Roosma

Mother Nature is very inspiring. Her greatest gifts are trees—big beautiful oak trees. I've spent numerous hours looking outside my son's window staring at a group of oak trees in our neighbor's backyard. I watch them bend and move with such grace and flexibility. Their roots are strong and grounded, and their leaves sway with the wind. Nothing uproots them as their trunks move side to side with such ease. I realized the beautiful oak trees I stared at while nursing my son for hours on end are a metaphor for who I wanted to become.

I'm a recovering perfectionist. I've lived my whole life trying to get that A+ no matter the hurt, disruption, or damage. My husband likes to say that when I get an A+ in one area of my life, I'm getting an F in another. Why didn't I listen to that advice sooner? I don't know. My husband is a wise man, so the mystery still remains, or is it no mystery at all. Someone who is a perfectionist doesn't like to think their way of doing something is ever wrong. That would insinuate that the perfectionist isn't perfect! I know—the nerve!

I thought perfectionism was the only answer; anything less than 110 percent wasn't good enough. After what felt like years, let me be honest, decades of this pattern, my body said, "Nope, you can't do this anymore." I gave birth to my daughter six years ago, and my postpartum journey was what brought the house down. I would frequently ask myself questions like, "Am I losing my mind? How can I feel this broken? Why can't my body just calm down?" My inner dialogue continued with: I feel trapped, stuck, the walls are crashing in.

I was in pieces and needed help in putting myself back together. Postpartum anxiety got me. It's amazing how our children are our biggest teachers. I tried to do it all, yep, you guessed it, I tried to be what I thought was the perfect mama—to be everything for my daughter. It turns out it was not a great idea and was super unsustainable.

I crawled my way out and healed, thankfully, with the help of my acupuncturist and Tiffany, who put this incredible book together. She introduced me to the spirit world. She opened my eyes and heart to trusting and believing in myself—believing that I have the answers within. I don't need to control every single thing in my life. I just need to listen to my intuition; that voice always has the answers, but we don't always hear it when life is busy and crazy. The voice is faint and subtle. It doesn't fight for attention, so you have to listen. I finally had faith in myself, faith that I was going to get through the hard times. Then, I got pregnant with my son.

My perfectionist tendencies made a grand reappearance after the birth of my son. It's funny how when you don't fully address something, it comes back and slaps you right across your face, so you have no option but to pay attention. The sting from the slap certainly hurts! The postpartum anxiety came back worse and partnered itself with insomnia. I tried to control everything as I did with my daughter, trying to be perfect, giving my son everything, and leaving nothing for myself. I was afraid that if I didn't do everything perfectly, I was somehow a bad mama and that my son wouldn't feel my love.

Then one day, I was so sleep-deprived because I wouldn't allow my husband to soothe our son at night, that I could barely keep my eyes open at the dinner table (I know, *I know*, ridiculous). And that was when it hit me. *How is this being a good mama? Why am I martyring myself for my child?*

That night I was short with my daughter and husband. "Cleanup your playroom. Feed the dog. Do I have to do everything?" My patience was wearing thin, and I wasn't allowing my family to help. All for what? For me to say, "I did it all and did it perfectly." What part of this is perfect? That night I let my husband take over. It was super hard for me to give up the reins, but I finally said, "Okay, we we'll do it your way." It turns out he's pretty smart and just all-around wonderful. I fed my son and then moved into our spare bedroom to sleep while my husband listened for him. I started doing this every night, and it turns out my son is better off for it! He's learning to self-soothe, not through crying it out—no judgment for those who have done that—but through playing with his hair and snuggling up to his raccoon we put in his crib to keep him company. Look what happens when I don't try to control—when I just let go and let it flow. It turns out my husband was right. I wonder how often I don't listen to him when I really should.

So the questions I needed to answer were: How do I give myself grace? How do I hold space for myself? How do I honor myself, my marriage, and my incredible children? Well, it sure isn't about being perfect. It's okay if I'm grumpy and my kids see that. My girlfriend said to me, "Don't you want your kids to know it's okay to make mistakes?" Of course! Whenever my daughter makes a mistake, we sit there and say, "Okay, that happened, so what did you learn from it? How can you do better next time?" There is no judgment from me when we talk about her mistake. We come at it with kindness and love. *So why was it so hard for me to make mistakes? And when I did, how come I couldn't be gentle with myself? Why am I so hard on myself?*

These are the questions I started to ask myself and continue to ask because we're never done learning how to be better and do better. When you think, *gosh, yeah, look at me, I got this whole life figured out, Spirit goes, that's hilarious, here is another lesson, and you better hold on.* With that, I have learned healing is not linear. You'll come out on top, but boy, are you going to see yourself fall and then have to pick yourself right back up to continue up the mountain. The peak is worth the hike, but don't forget the journey. The journey is where you learn about yourself and your patterns.

I don't know about you, but I started to realize my perfectionism meant I was lying all the time. And I mean all the time. Throughout the day, I found myself in lie after lie. I wasn't trying to hurt anyone. My intention with lying wasn't to upset the person. I did it because a lie would make it seem like I was still perfect—I didn't drop the ball. "So sorry Terry, please excuse my delay, I forgot to email you back, I was busy this weekend with home improvements." But the reality was there were no home improvements. I would make up lies as to why I couldn't go to dinner that night when in actuality, I just didn't want to go out!

I am a homebody. Then, about two years ago, I started to see my pattern. I began to see how much I lied and how bad that felt. I wasn't truthful with people, but more importantly, I wasn't truthful with myself. I realized I lied because I didn't like the judgment when I told the truth. I didn't like when people were disappointed in me; I didn't like when people saw my flaws, and I didn't want to let anyone I loved down. How silly is that? I can't live in fear of what others think of me. I have to speak my truth. Telling the truth is freedom, and it gives me strength. I live a more courageous life, a life where I can be my authentic self. And, do you know how hard it is to remember all your lies? Talk about wasted energy. Sure, there is still the occasional white lie when it comes to my kids. "Yes, I love that drawing, thank you." But other than that, Mama doesn't lie.

I bet you're wondering when I will explain the oak trees I spoke about. While on my healing journey, I started noticing how much I wanted to live my life like a tree. Big beautiful oak trees are my tree of choice. I'm a visual person. I need something for my mind to reference when I see myself slipping back into my perfectionist tendencies. And for me, that's a tree.

Whenever I feel myself trying to control a situation, I relax my body, take a deep breath and start to move like a tree. I picture one of the oak trees outside my son's window on a windy day. I see it swaying back and forth with no effort, just doing what it was made to do. I slowly and thoughtfully move like the oak tree, swaying side to side. This movement not only calms me down, but the gentle flow of my body reminds me that life isn't fluid and when challenging things come up, or when I see myself needing that A+, I need to surrender my thoughts and feelings and let go. I need to stop resisting, tensing, planning my next move or action, and just sit back and observe my thought pattern. I then picture my feet as roots, grounded deep into the Earth's core. I then recite, "My roots are strong, solid, and sturdy. Nothing is going to uproot me, and I'm not going to topple over. I've got this!"

Ever since I started doing this, I've noticed I'm no longer frustrated. When I flow with life instead of fighting it, everything seems to get a little easier. I'm no longer disappointed or need to be perfect because I'm living in the moment. I'm being mindful of the situation and not making assumptions. I have also found that going for a walk is one of the best ways to change my perspective when I need to let go of something that isn't serving me. For me, nothing beats feeling the glorious sun on my face, listening to the sounds of birds chirping, smelling flowers, or simply putting my bare feet on our grass. The grounding energy the soil provides me takes me from scatter-brained to calm and mindful in minutes. My daughter will even come outside with me! "Oh, Mommy, let's ground together. I feel good energy, and my body is calm." I love her enthusiasm and zest for life!

And, as a side note, have you ever stopped to look at a bird, like, really watched a bird? Sometimes I sit on my front porch and wait for birds to fly by: Cardinals, blue jays, and yellow finches! Their colors are absolutely stunning. No crayon can ever match the gorgeous color of their feathers. Mother Nature makes no mistakes! But if she did, I'm sure she'd roll with it and not get hung up on being perfect.

Along with glorious Mother Nature and her infinite wisdom, I've found meditation amazingly helpful in my healing journey. To be honest, this one hasn't been easy for me. I've practiced meditation on and off, more off than on, but I have found it again, and I'm hopeful I'll stick with it this time. I'm not putting too much pressure on myself to have a perfect practice. I'm learning! I've also been told there's no such thing as a perfect practice. Everyone's practice looks different. After my daughter was born, I took an Introduction to Meditation class at Stanford University. That was the first time I started meditating on a daily basis. I found my thoughts clearer, anxiety lessened, and my body felt calm. Unfortunately, as I entered a stressful part of my life, my meditation practice slipped away when we moved across the country. I found myself going back to meditation here and there, but it wasn't until before my son was born that I really paid attention to the need to meditate.

My son was eight days past his due date, and I felt pretty uncomfortable! His weight after birth was nine pounds, five ounces, so you can imagine how I was over lugging him around. I had an overwhelming feeling, like when a wave crashes the sand, that I needed to mediate. I felt like there was something I needed to release, something I had to let go of in order to stimulate labor. I sat on my couch and started to meditate. What I experienced was one of the most profound and incredible experiences of my life. It reaffirmed my connection to Spirit. I quietly and gently repeated, "Let go, let go, let go." I started to see colors—that's when I know I'm connected to Spirit. Suddenly, I felt a burst of energy shoot down my left and right side. The energy started below my armpit and stopped at my hips. I felt my son physically move further down into my pelvis, just like that! And I went into labor hours later. Whenever I question if Spirit is real, I recall this experience, and it re-energizes me.

Visualization and meditation aren't the only tools I've used to help overcome my perfectionism. Journaling and practicing gratitude are two of my other favorites. I know, so clique, but it's the truth! I never thought of myself as a writer. Writing in a journal felt intimidating and cumbersome. I always thought keeping a diary was for creative people, real writers, and not for me. I listened to a podcast, and the woman being interviewed spoke of her journey to find inner peace. "Writing down my thoughts was a huge part of my recovery. You have to find the time in your busy schedule and go from there."

So, that day, I challenged myself to pick up a pen and start writing. The prompt was only to write one page, and it could be about anything. It turned out that one page was not enough for all the thoughts I had that day. Ever since then, I find it incredible how I can sit down with my journal, not knowing where to start and end up solving the unsolvable. Writing organizes my thoughts and puts my feelings into words I normally can't articulate. I've solved many of my plaguing problems with just a pen and paper, and might I suggest going to your local papery and supporting them by buying a pen and a beautiful journal? Nothing like feeling a pen flow effortlessly across paper.

When you're writing down your deepest thoughts, you discover negativity has no place in your life. Negativity is a waste of space and time, and when I realized this, I came to the conclusion that positivity and practicing gratitude were the only way to go. If I find myself grumpy, stuck, or inflexible, I reframe my thoughts. I might be annoyed that I had trouble sleeping the night before, so I will say to myself, *but gosh, I'm so grateful for a warm bed, clean sheets, and a safe place to rest my body.* I know it sounds simple but changing the narrative does retrain your neuropathways.

Over the last two years, when I've needed encouragement to stop focusing on the negative, that was when I started seeing repeating numbers throughout my day: 222, 333, 444, 555. I didn't know it then, but that was Spirit communicating with me. They are called angel numbers, and the sequences all have meanings. Once I understand the meaning of a certain combination, I sit back, nodding my head because the advice from the angels was exactly what I needed to hear. I just looked at the time and saw 333. Wow, if that isn't a sign!

In conclusion, I certainly don't have all the answers. I'm still a work in progress, but what I can say is that now I have tools to help me when life throws curve balls. When the unexpected happens, I stop, breathe, and listen to my intuition. My faith in Spirit and myself helped me realize perfectionism is no longer a viable path, and I'm in charge of my destiny.

Kate was born in Northern California. She spent most of her childhood hanging out with her brother and playing basketball.

She graduated from Loyola Marymount University in Southern California with a Sociology degree and then moved to Chicago, Illinois. There, she met the most influential person in her life, her husband. While in Chicago, she graduated from Rush University with a Master's Degree in Nursing. Her internship was in labor and delivery. During her schooling and internship, she realized that although Western medicine has a time and place, it wasn't what she wanted to practice. After moving to New York State for her husband's graduate degree, she turned down a nursing position. In the small town of Ithaca, she found her love for stationery and managed a papery for the two years she was living there.

Her love for all things holistic opened the door for her to become a doula and then, many years later, have a home birth. She will be fulfilling her dream of becoming an acupuncturist by getting her Doctorate of Oriental Medicine (DOM) next year.

She enjoys reading non-fiction, spending time with loved ones, and being outside in nature in her free time. She and her husband have two incredible children, a sweet rescue dog, and now live in Maryland.

CHAPTER 3

THE CYCLES OF GAIA AND THE RISE OF THE DIVINE FEMININE

HEALING THE WOUNDS OF DUALITY

Vila Donovan, L.Ac.

I was born free into a utopian bubble where dreams come true. Well, not exactly, but Los Angeles was the land of the free for my generation. It was a world where creativity ruled, and religious dogma had no place.

As Jewish immigrants, my mother's family worshiped at the altar of civil rights, and as Irish immigrants, my father's family prayed for surf.

My paternal grandmother came to Los Angeles from Chicago in the 1930s to be an actress. She was a talented swimmer and found success in the stunt department and began her career as a Busby Berkley girl and a Bathing Beauty where she doubled Esther Williams. My grandmother's first husband and my biological grandfather played for the minor leagues as a Los Angeles Angel, but the man who raised my father and whom I knew as my grandfather was her third husband. They met on the set of the Tarzan TV series where she doubled Maureen O' Sullivan as Jane, and he doubled Johnny Weissmuller as Tarzan.

My grandmother's name was Mary, and the name suited her, for she was the kindest, sweetest, loveliest person you would ever meet. She was Catholic, and her belief in God was profound, but religion in Hollywood was a nuisance. By 1950 she would be divorced twice, married three times, and excommunicated from the Catholic Church.

But my grandmother's belief in God had little dependence upon the opinions or rules of the church. It was she who instilled within me a relationship with spirit (whom she knew as Jesus), a relationship that was free, dependent on no one, and unconditional.

My mother was the first generation of single moms. She and her peers celebrated the arrival of the pill and Roe V. Wade. My mother burned her bra, took LSD, started her own business, and made her way without the aid of a husband. She went to the Monterey Pop Festival and raised me to be free-thinking and self-reliant. One evening, when I was sixteen, my mother taught me to read tarot cards. "Let me give you a reading," My mother said as we sat down on my pink flowered bed spread. She shuffled the cards and laid them out. The beautifully colored cards looked like stained glass and I fell into the pictures as she told me my fortune. I don't recall what she said, but I do recall the name of the deck, it was the Aquarian deck. The next day she took me to a psychic store in Venice and bought me my first deck of cards. The tarot opened my life and mind to the wondrous world of symbolism, intuition, and magic. The tarot taught me self-reflection and not to fear my shadow but heal it. These first steps would guide my path forward into a discovery of ancient goddess religions, earth magic, and Fairy Wicca.

For me, it was never about spells, incantations, bending anything to my influence or desires, but about wisdom and trust, nature and the cycles of the Earth (Gaia), and the movement of celestial bodies. It was and is about being in harmony with the planet and diving into the effortlessly flowing river of energy I call grace. It is natural law and the spiritual law of attraction. It is science, and the awareness of the sentient nature of all things, not just humans. It is the wisdom of the goddess and the divine feminine. It is a remembering of a time when men did not rule the universe.

This wisdom would inspire me to become a healer. I chose a degree in Chinese Medicine. I earned my master's degree when I was 29 and opened a practice in Monterey, California. My career as an acupuncturist was effortless, but it was my own healing that still lay hidden in the depths of my subconscious—a shadow that lurked, following along behind me until I would be forced to look it square in the eye.

By my 30s, I realized I had an issue with being bullied. I would struggle for years. One situation after another would manifest for me. No matter my strength, talent, and success, I'd crumble and dissolve before any bully, handing over my dreams, hard work, and walking away. It mystified me for years as I searched for the reasons behind my vulnerability. It was the greatest pain of my life, and I searched for a solution. The answers I sought would eventually be illuminated by the light of the moon and on the beaches of a tropical paradise.

In 2012 my partner's job changed, and we moved to Hawaii. This would be the second time in my life I'd move to Hawaii. The first time was in 1974 when I was three. My parents divorced when I was two, and a year later, my mother and I moved to the island of Maui.

In Hawaii, I experienced something called Kill Haole Day, a Hawaiian norm that meant, "Today you beat the shit out of any non-local person you come across." The Hawaiian people had their land stolen, and they were angry. I would discover just how angry. By the time I was of school age and out of the sight of my mother, I experienced physical assaults by adults and kids twice my age.

Our time in Hawaii lasted only three years, but those years left their mark. When we returned to California, I was seven, which was a welcome change for me, but I was not like other kids. I had severe anxiety, and the trauma of violence left me so shaken and insecure I found every day a challenge. In school, I excelled academically, but that success garnered attention from a bully, and the whole situation felt like life or death to me. My body remembered well what happened in Hawaii, and no matter how many people told me I was safe, my body told me otherwise.

My experience in Hawaii compounded an already established pain-body I inherited from my maternal ancestral line. I had an active pain-body of trauma that lay in the collective past of my Jewish ancestors, who endured thousands of years of racism and prejudice, and my own experiences of racial violence in Hawaii, where the pain of colonization was so acute it manifested as physical assaults.

My own healing would lie not just in my own past but the collective past wounding of the testosterone-driven patriarchal system that has enslaved, oppressed, colonized, waged war, and traumatized our planet for thousands of years.

I learned that trauma and violence, whether physical, psychological, or emotional, changes our brain and body chemistry. My body was still in survival mode and had been for decades.

This is where my healing began. My mind could not heal when my body was in an active state of post-traumatic stress. As an acupuncturist and bodyworker, I learned to let my mind rest and approach my healing by re-establishing a healthy endocrine system. By rebalancing my fight or flight hormones and giving my physical body the opportunity to remember what it feels like to be out of fight or flight, I could begin to change my responses to stress and triggers. For me, this came with the practice of alternate breathing techniques, which can lower cortisol levels to zero if done for ten minutes a day. Once my body was calm, my mind could follow. When my mind and body joined together in this quiet place, I could journey deep into the wisdom of the goddess and find answers to our collective past and to the healing of the planet itself. One afternoon while sitting in this quiet place, I felt a presence enter the room. A voice spoke to me in my mind and said, *I am from the future. I am a healer like you. I come from a planet of healers. Know that the healers of Earth are part of a larger network of healers that exist throughout the galaxy.* The presence which seemed decidedly female then asked, *Would you like a healing?*

"Yes," I said, and she merged with me, bringing with her purple and blue lights that spun inside and outside of me. After a minute or two the spinning stopped and settled, leaving me feeling vibrant and balanced in a way I had not felt before. A sense of wellbeing came over me as she moved away.

As she departed I heard her say, *Call on me anytime you need, I am always here, for I am a future version of you.*

So let us travel back in time to the beginning, not my beginning, but our collective beginning. Let's journey back 300 thousand years to the times of Lemuria, and forward from there 150 thousand years to the inception of Atlantis and the joining together of these two great societies—one ruled by the divine feminine and one ruled by the divine masculine. Lemuria was a graceful goddess-centered culture, and Atlantis was a male-driven active culture—both beautiful and majestic in their ideals.

In the beginning, the dream of Atlantis was that it would be an integrated and balanced society, but as the Atlantean peoples explored more and more duality, the integrated society began to break down, ultimately resulting in the ripping apart of the divine feminine and divine masculine principles in the consciousness of this great global society. A timeline emerged dominated by a male-driven agenda, and the goddess was all but forgotten.

After the fall of Atlantis, these systems were re-established in our world and peaked in the times of Rome and the holy inquisition, leading to the burning of witches and complete suppression of the goddess, marking the darkest times in our world. These are the wounds we carry within us to this day. It's the collective trauma asking to be healed at this time. But these patriarchal energies are now in decline, and the goddess is on the rise. The god and goddess are asking to be reunited in all of their glory as a unified, balanced consciousness.

This is not a denial of the masculine but a healing of these wounds and a reintegration of the two polarities—a bonding and merging of duality in its most primal form, consciousness. This consciousness is what the planet (Gaia) is advocating for us all now.

Earth, or Gaia, has her own astronomical cycle of 26 thousand years. Every 26 thousand years, the Earth's North Pole returns to the same star; this is called precession. This 26 thousand-year cycle is broken down into two 13 thousand-year cycles—13 thousand years of integration ruled by the divine feminine and 13 thousand years of disintegration ruled by the divine masculine. The Mayan, Hindu, and Egyptian calendars break these cycles into ages. Golden Age, Silver Age, Bronze Age, and Iron Age. It's now at the dawning of the Age of Aquarius and the end of the Mayan calendar in 2012 that we upon this Earth and the planet itself embark upon a 13-thousand-year cycle of integration. This is a time of great healing, for the great wheel has turned, and Gaia (Earth) moves towards a new golden era, but this time is unique because it's not a shift from masculine to feminine but a reintegration of the divine feminine and divine masculine, led by the heartbeat of the great mother.

If you're here now, you are to be a part of this great reunification and bring the goddess back into the world so she can lead the shift into fourth-density heart chakra consciousness. This is what is meant by the popular concept of a fifth-dimensional shift.

I invite you to light a candle, plant some rosemary, and find your personal magic. Let the great mother and the fairies and the wondrous world of your imagination and bliss move you into the river of grace, and may your life flow effortlessly to your heart's desire, for this is the blessing of integration. Welcome the Great Mother as she makes her ascent back into the front of the consciousness of this world and leads the planet back into a new golden age.

I invite you to remember the immortality of your soul and the vastness of experiences you've had, and I invite you to be here now and to breathe and to heal. By bringing our physical bodies out of fight or flight, we heal the traumas of our collective past. Within the realms of deep relaxation, we re-align our chemistry and break the cycles of stress and trauma. It begins with each of us—wise women and wise men on our personal journey.

My personal healing is ongoing as I learn that I do not need to be afraid. I make better choices now and recognize the situations and relationships that leave me feeling unsafe or stressed.

Indulge in whatever healing modalities you're drawn to and know that the cycles of Gaia, the planet we're on, are supporting this reintegration of female and male principles in our consciousness. Now is the time of the wise woman; it's the return of the goddess and the great mother, and it's the rise of the divine feminine.

Vila has over 20 years of experience as an acupuncturist and herbalist and over 30 years of experience as a Tarot reader and psychic. She received her master's degree in Chinese medicine in 2000 from Five Braches University in Santa Cruz, California. Her acupuncture treatments include a combination of gentle acupuncture, acutonics (sound healing using tuning forks instead of needles), and Internal Medicine specialties that include women's health hormone balancing for women of all ages, gut health, balancing of the emotional body, and deep relaxation treatments.

Her Psychic services include Tarot readings, angel, spirit guide, and fairy readings. Galactic services include galactic history sessions, galactic lineage sessions, and galactic healings for ancestral trauma.

You can find all the details for her acupuncture and psychic services or make an appointment at:

Website: www.viladonovan.com
Email: viladonovan@yahoo.com
Facebook: You can follow her @lady of the mountain center for galactic consciousness on Facebook and see Vila's free weekly updates and tarot readings.

Acupuncture services are available in Ojai, California.
Psychic services are available everywhere, remote.
Books: *Find Your Voice Save Your Life Book 3,* available on amazon.

Visit us at www.viladonovan.com for the release date of her novel *The Vila, The story of Lemuria, and those who come from the sea.*

CHAPTER 4

TRUSTING THE NUDGES

A CORPORATE RESEARCHER'S JOURNEY CONNECTING WITH HER PSYCHIC MEDIUMSHIP ABILITIES

Bonnie Casamassima, MFA,
Research Professor, Evidential Medium

Click. The door closes on the corporate research world behind me. *Ahh, alone at last.* A rarity and dream for the introvert in me. Silence fills the 8'x8' green-walled conference room. I booked 30 minutes in here over my lunch break to try this thing called meditation. My attention turns to the tiny window overlooking the trees blowing in the wind. I take a deep breath and exhale. The corporate frenzy is just beyond these four green walls and a thin wooden door. *I could kiss you, sweet door, and the privacy you create.* Passing my hands across the gray upholstered chair, I sit and instantly feel held. It's a busy time at work. It's always a busy time at work. Maybe one day, it'll get calmer *if I could just finish this one more thing.* I find myself working 60+ hours each week—every week.

I'm exhausted. I'm drained. It's all I can do to drag myself out of bed each morning. I feel dim and depressed at times. It's my normal mode. Each day I lather, rinse, and repeat.

I remember hearing about meditation from a friend. The conversation was about how it helped her reduce stress. I remember thinking, *Meditation? I don't have time for that.* I'm too busy. Plus, as I'll later realize, being busy equaled being important. I've lived this way my whole life, so I think I'll keep being importa. . . I mean busy. Yet still, I'm stressed. I often feel so drained. I can't help but think *there's gotta be a better way.*

Back in the sacred solitude of that green-walled conference room, meditation feels a bit more possible. It's a whole new world to me, but I'm working on being more open, so I try it. I searched online and found a two-minute guided meditation video and press play. *Okay, two minutes, I could justify dedicating two minutes to this, well, two minutes plus the five-second ad. Ha!* I close my eyes, slide in my headphones, settle into the gray upholstered chair, and begin.

"Inhale."

"Hold."

"Exhale."

"Hold."

Two minutes feels like an eternity. In those two minutes, I must have had hundreds of thoughts fly through my mind. *Is this even working? What does working even mean?* Despite the questioning, I can't help but feel a bit more at peace. A tiny bit more—centered—*is that a word to use here?* Without overthinking it (a very foreign concept for my analytical researcher mind), I acknowledge that something about it feels right. Something about the experience is pulling me to try it again. I'm not sure what the right feeling is, but I'm working on being more open, so I go with it. I book the same 8x8 green-walled conference room for the next day.

Click. Door closed. *Ahh,* settle, deep breaths, repeat.

Today, successful completion of a three-minute video! It focused on grounding and pulling my energy back into my body. *What is this talk about energy?* I'm curious, feeling that same nudge I felt yesterday, so I book the room for a third day.

Each time I show up, feel that nudge and follow it. That nudge keeps leading me to feel more at peace. My work schedule is still the same, but my state of being is somehow different. I think, where was meditation when I was in graduate school researching around the clock and constantly pulling all-nighters running myself ragged? In reality, meditation was right there all along. The nudges were too. I was just choosing not to focus my energy there, choosing instead to focus on the grind.

I find the nudges to be like a muscle. The more I listen, the stronger and clearer they feel. Each time I follow those whole-body yeses, it's as if I'm connecting more with my deeper self. It feels healthy, and I feel lighter, so I continue to trust the crumbs of the journey.

Then one day, during meditation, something happened that changed the course of my life forever.

I was alone at my house settling into mediation. I found a binaural beat track online listed to be the same frequency as the human heart. I think, *Sure, I'll try it* and press play.

"Inhale"

"Hold"

"Exhale"

"Hold"

I settle in and calm my energy.

Bam! A moving picture of a woman jumps into my sight—only my eyes are closed! It's hard to explain, really, but the moving picture was not from me, but it was as if it was coming through me. The woman had kind eyes, a huge smile, and a familiar sense like we knew each other. Only I'd not met her in my lifetime. The visual was powerful, and it scared the living crap out of me!

I physically jumped back in my seat. My eyes flew open, the picture dissipated, and I shook my head in disbelief. *What the heck was that?* I mean I had dreams before, and this was kind of like that, but it was different. It *felt* different.

Am I losing my mind here? I'd spent the past decade-plus working in the analytical research fields of academia and the corporate world. On top of that, I'd grown up in a very conservative area that saw anything that was not a white man wearing old-school Birkenstock shoes with long brown hair and blue eyes as evil. Well, this was *definitely* not that, so was it evil? I freaked out and decided not to tell anyone out of fear of judgment.

Days went by, and yet, I could not shake the experience. It was so powerful. I felt incredible in those brief split seconds when the familiar woman appeared. It was as if my heart and body expanded beyond the constraints of the boundaries of my skin. I felt held, calm, and such powerful love for those brief split seconds. In reflection, I noticed that it was only when I switched out of my heart and into my mind, that I freaked out.

I finally got up the courage to tell my partner about the experience and then a good friend I knew from the corporate world who also meditated. I'm so glad I did. They held space for me and my friend said, "Bonnie, you're not losing your mind. You're connecting with your intuition!"

"My what?"

"Your intuition. You know, that internal guidance that people like Steve Jobs, Einstein, and Nicolas Tesla talk about using. Here, if you're open to it, book a session with this medium I go to."

"A medium? Like Ms. Cleo?" I said. "I don't know if I believe all of that really, but I trust you, and I'm trying to be more open."

"If you have a curiosity, a nudge as you call them—then think about trying out a session."

"Okay," I said, "I'll be open and try it."

I trusted the nudge of wanting to test out a channeling session, so I went to her website and booked a time before I could overthink it.

I showed up to the call admittedly a bit skeptical and guarded, yet I tried to be open.

"Do you have any specific questions you'd like to ask?" The medium asked.

"I'd like to be open and just see what's coming through." I said. "Would that be okay?"

"Sure, let me connect with your guides." After a brief pause, she continued. "I see you as a little girl crying because of something that happened in the garden. Something about weeds, and you just wanted to play. There's anger and sadness. Your guides are saying this is important because you're being asked to go in and release this memory. Forgive it and all involved. It's coming up in your life now as an energetic block. You can't work and have fun while doing it. It's leading to you overwork."

I thought, *How does she know this? There's no way she'd know this. I've not thought about that memory for years!*

"Wow," I said. "That's amazing and makes a lot of sense. Are they guiding me on how to do that? What did you say, release?"

The medium translated instructions for a meditation for me to do as homework after our session.

It felt aligned, so I trusted it and went into the memory during meditation to see what my younger self needed—tears streamed down my face, and my heart pulsed deeply. My younger self asked to be held. She asked to be told it was ok to play and have fun. My mother also appeared in the meditation. She wanted to play as well, and her anger had been a projection of that. Tears streamed down both our faces. We hugged and cried together. Tears of release. Tears of freedom from the energy we'd subconsciously been holding as chains limiting us in our physical lives from more happiness, growth, and joy.

After I came out of that experience in meditation, I felt lighter.

Trusting the nudges continued to lead me to experiences of more energy and peace, so I kept following them. I kept trusting my gut even when I thought they were strange. Suppose it felt right in my body. If it felt grounded, calm, and present—I went with it and followed the bread crumbs.

For example, around the same time as my first session with a medium, I was sitting down to eat dinner at a friend's wedding. I sat next to a woman I knew peripherally but not very well. So, there we were, sitting at this beautiful wedding when I got the urge to ask her, *Have you ever seen ghosts?* In my mind, I remember thinking, *What? I'm not asking her that. I don't even know her, and we're at this wedding, and that's the first thing I'll ask her. Um, nope!* The nudge was so strong, so nevertheless, I followed. I trusted. Bracing myself to be looked at like I had seven heads, I followed the nudge and asked.

"So, I know this might sound weird and out of the blue, but I'm feeling pulled to ask you this, and I've been working on being more open to trusting my pulls or nudges. A few months ago, just as I was about to fall asleep, I saw a figure standing in my bedroom doorway. It was about seven feet tall and looked as if it was coming through a screen. I remember not being asleep yet, but I was not fully awake. Obviously, the visual stood out to me, but what stood out even more, was how I felt when it appeared. I was so calm and grounded. It was as if they wanted to tell me something, but they spoke no words. I just sort of knew they wanted to talk to me—if that makes any sense. So anyway, I know this is super random, but I'm feeling the pull to ask if something like that has ever happened to you?"

Was she staring at me as if I had seven heads?

I felt my face and body start to brace for ridicule.

Instead, she said, "Umm…what? Yes! How did you know? Only mine was in my kitchen. I was just standing there wiping my counter, and then two large figures appeared—they were kind of. . ."

We said at the same time, "Translucent, but you could see them!"

Again, at the same time we exclaimed, "yes!"

I was blown away! We then went on to share other stories of our experiences. We became very close, after that day, and supported each other on our journeys connecting with our intuitive mediumship abilities.

Even with these powerful experiences, the analytical researcher in me needed more proof. By that time, I'd moved from the corporate world into the world of academia as a professor guiding graduate students' research. I felt as if I was living in two worlds, one filled with following the magical nudges of strengthening my intuitive connection, the other filled with data analysis, spreadsheets, and strict research protocol.

This analytical approach is most likely what guided me to do what I did next. Still holding resistance to the magic that was unfolding every time I trusted the nudge, I booked two separate sessions with two separate mediums on the same day. One session was in the morning, and the other session was that same night.

I went into both sessions with a wide-open mind—no specific questions. I shared nothing as far as goals with either one, and was open to seeing what came through. Then, as you've likely guessed, the same information came through from both physic mediums! Mind you; these two separate people were in different geographical locations. As far as I know, they did not know each other, and I certainly did not tell either of them about the other's session.

They shared that I was being shown a path forward to pursue training to develop and hone my intuitive abilities. They both said there'd be a monetary and time investment involved, and I'd know what step to take next. They both affirmed, "Keep following your nudges."

I had a million questions. Yet still, I responded, "Okay, I'll follow the nudges to see what comes up to pursue this. Thank you for your guidance and time." Leaving the sessions, I was shocked at the consistency of the messages, yet still unsure of what to do next. My mind began racing: *Is there even training for honing your intuition? Where would I even start looking for this? What would I type into Google? How would I know if the information is accurate?* I decided to just release control of the outcome and do what I've been being more open to doing—trusting the nudges.

The *very* next day, I was scrolling through Facebook, and up popped a video of Jamie Butler, a wonderful woman I'd met in Atlanta while giving a research presentation. She's a natural-born medium and had been practicing for over three decades. As she talked, I could not believe my ears. She shared that she was launching a six-month program the following month. Get this!

To

help

people

connect

with

their

intuition!

Tingles filled my body. An affirmation I'd learned to listen to throughout this period. Before I could overthink it, I followed the nudge, wrote a note of my interest in joining, and pressed send.

I remember sitting there wondering what the heck I'd just done. *I'm a researcher. I'm a corporate world person. I wear suits and heels. And a piece of me really likes those things. Does this mean I need to move to a mountain top and meditate all day?*

Regardless, I followed the nudge. I got accepted. The program was phenomenal and it changed my life.

There were weekly assignments to practice our deepened intuitive connections with others as part of the mentorship. By then, the visuals were coming stronger in meditation. I was using them as tools to guide my journey with work projects, in the way I taught, and when making life decisions.

Then one day, a visual popped in to do a channeling session over zoom for a friend. Before thinking twice about it, I sent her a message asking if she'd like to try it out. She replied instantly with, "heck yes!" We got on a zoom call, and over the next two hours, I shared the clear visuals that came through from her guides to her. Advice from career projects to love interests to where she was being called to move all came through. It was powerful for her. I felt weightless and pure love. It's as if both our feet did not touch the ground for a week.

Pan forward nearly three years, I'm awestruck at the life changes that came from following that single nudge. From going through another powerful love-filled mentorship training led by incredible souls-Moonrise, to building a community, following the nudges is an everyday necessity.

At the time of writing these words, trusting that pull has led me to the honor of supporting over a hundred incredible clients with their own channeling sessions

The information that flows through in each session is unique. Often insights can range from dream-like metaphors to specific detailed action steps. Such as in one session, a woman connected asking, "What was coming through to her about a work project?" As we began, a clear image of the book she was to write instantly appeared. That image was followed by a frenzy of vivid rapid-fire visuals showing the range of people who'd be supported by her writing. The session closed after a detailed outline of each chapter came through for her. It was truly amazing.

Or another session where an incredible client shared, "It's my first time having a session, and I'm a bit nervous. But I'm curious, can we connect with my Dad?" Instantly her warm, gentle, and so proud Dad came through. I shared, "He's handing you a bouquet of yellow daisies and wants to know if you'd like them?" Love rushed through all of us instantly. Tears streamed down our faces. The client goes on to share, "Those were my Dad's favorite flowers!" The flowers were his way of confirming it was him with her and giving her comfort. He then shared ways they could continue to connect beyond the session. He closed by affirming, "Yes, it's me you're feeling as tingles resting on your left shoulder in moments where you miss my support." She could trust her own intuition in their powerful connection.

It's hard to express how much of an honor it is to hold space and support such incredible people. Each session is unique, seeming to meet each person exactly where they are on their own path. Often the sessions, like my first one with a medium did for me, leave the clients with an affirmation knowing they're already connected to their own deepening intuitive abilities. They're clear on their next steps and trust their own nudges even more. After powerful experiences like these, the pull to share my mediumship abilities openly with the world outweighed the fear I was using to keep myself quiet.

I never expected to get in touch with my psychic intuition the day I escaped into that conference room to try this thing called meditation, but something nudged me there. I'm so happy I followed the nudge and continue to do so each day.

Trusting the nudges has been such a powerful part for my own journey. I've created a support tool to help people identify and follow their own nudges. If nurturing, please visit www.intuitivebynature.com/trustingthenudges to download your own activity book with prompts and guidance.

Cheers to your journey and trusting your nudges more fully along the way.

With love,
Bonnie

Bonnie Casamassima is an Evidential Medium, researcher, and speaker. She supports you through intuitive channeling, and through research-driven education to help foster connecting with our intuitive abilities in our everyday modern lives. She holds a Bachelor of Science and a Master of Fine Arts degree, as well as a six-month Intuitive Certification Program with Jamie Butler and a year-long shaman-led training, Moonrise, by Wild Sage Healing Arts. She enjoys time with her partner and his two incredible kids, live music, dancing, and a good belly laugh. You can find out more at www.intuitivebynature.com.

CHAPTER 5

HEALING THROUGH DIVORCE

HOW TO PART WAYS AND STAY ON A JOURNEY OF LOVE

Ana Claudia Palla, Ph.D.

We are taught that to divorce is to separate, disconnect, and set ourselves apart from life as a couple. We expect it will bring a lot of fighting, pain, and suffering. In my case, it brought unity, integration, connection, and balance instead.

It was January 13, 2021 when Bill, my husband of 16 years, and I said yes to our divorce. Only we could know the pain and struggles we lived with on a daily basis. We were mirrors of each other's shadows for all those years. Our marriage amplified a sense of rejection and unworthiness we both experienced in our childhood. We could not bear who we were with each other and the growing impact on our young seven-year-old daughter Maya. We needed to set ourselves apart from all the nonsense.

My mother, Marlene, was my biggest supporter. Long ago, she welcomed me into her womb during the most frightening period of her life. My older brother was born ten months earlier with a disability in both of his feet. She worried about the second child she carried.

It was a full moon and the first lunar eclipse of 1976. On May 13 in Sao Paulo, Brazil, Dr. Nelson declares: "Look, Marlene, it's a beautiful girl, and she's perfect!" All the fears of having another disabled child—the burden, shame, and guilt I experienced in the womb—were gone in a moment. Tears of joy and a big sigh of relief came through her breast milk.

Has my entire life been about going back to that blissful experience at my mother's breast?

My parents had the four of us in less than four years. Both worked long hours. Home could be stressful. The culture in Brazil is to be thin. I was not. I was prescribed my first diet by an endocrinologist at age seven.

The bullying by my siblings and corrections by my parents at the table was a constant humiliation. I became good at lying, cheating, hiding, and eating as fast as I could to avoid the comments and ridicule. Hundreds of times, I left the table upset.

My worth was determined by how much I weighed or how successful I was on a diet. I've been in this vicious cycle many times in my life. I invested time and money in seminars and transformational programs, intending to fix myself. I worked very hard, lost the weight, and then gained it back. It was never enough.

Hard work was one of the biggest values inherited from the generations of immigrants in our family. Both of my parents needed to work full-time to meet our budget needs. We took one simple vacation each year.

We traveled by car to the south of Brazil to visit my dad's family. It was the highlight of our year. Dad strapped our luggage to the roof and made a bed on the back of the van for the four of us. The 12 to 16-hour trip was an adventure. From singing Italian music, eating snacks, Dad bribing the cops, and the stress of escaping near-collisions on the single-lane roads full of trucks, we finally arrived at the farm of Nono and Nona, our Italian grandparents.

We were treated like rock stars: "Our relatives from Sao Paulo are arriving!" They offered a table full of homemade juice, milk, jelly, cheese, salami, and bread. We were immediately barefoot and free to run and play with the animals at the creek and walk long distances to get some clear quartz. It was a paradise, and I was free to eat whatever I wanted!

Back home, I was good at school, but I didn't have many friends and no boyfriends. I had my first period when I was 9. By 11, I was at my full height and tallest in my class. I could defend myself. But I hated it every time I got angry and aggressive.

My daily struggle was the constant experience of not being accepted, trying to meet others' expectations, and never feeling good enough. I isolated myself, and I would not accept invitations to go out with friends, birthday parties, or even play on the street. However, as a tall and strong teen, I found my expression in playing competitive volleyball. I played for many years but quit from the fear of being cut after changing team levels. I was disappointed in myself and grew to 225 pounds.

My dad experienced disease, depression, and cancer throughout his life. Around the same time I quit playing volleyball, he lost his job after complications from back surgery.

We moved to a public school inside a Catholic institution for children with disabilities. I quickly became friends with the disabled in my class. I volunteered at the physical therapy clinic attached to the school. I spent all my free time there.

I suddenly had a purpose. The focus and context of my life shifted. I was there helping the poor, abandoned, and disabled. That experience gave me a new perspective. I felt proud of whom I was becoming and grateful for my parents and family. I belonged there, and I was loved and valued. My weight did not matter, and my internal dialog shifted. Making a difference was more important than my self-pity.

When it was time to go to college, I knew I wanted to work with people with disabilities. I was admitted to Sao Paulo State University, a free public university two hours from home, as a physical education major. I could not wait to get out of the house!

I was doing great on my work and academics. As a freshman, I started volunteering in many community-based extension programs, including one for kids with severe disabilities. I was shaken by the experience of bulimia and was grateful to learn a lot from a therapist to stop and manage the behavior.

The day after I defended my Master's degree dissertation, I left Brazil to work as a nanny for three kids in New York City. All I would need is to learn English to pursue a Ph.D. in the US. I left for New York City with one small suitcase, little money, and a return ticket. I knew I could return home if something didn't work out.

I came from a family of immigrants from Portugal on Mom's side and Italy from Dad's. They all left Europe during WW II, seeking a better life in Brazil. I inherited their strength and resilience to overcome the challenges in the US.

But I was insecure about having relationships with men. All my long-term relationships were with non-threatening men. And each time, they were a mirror of my ongoing struggles. We would rely on each other for our unmet emotional needs. Dissatisfied, I would stay in relationships for years until I had a good enough excuse to break up.

During my time in New York City, I had a relationship with Larry. The terrorist attacks of 9-11 gave me the excuse I needed to return to Brazil, but I didn't have the courage to break up with him. Larry called me every day for six months. Over the phone, I ended the relationship just before returning to the US.

I received a fellowship for a Ph.D. program at the University of Virginia, and my first year was difficult. The anxiety and struggles with my English were excruciating, and the adjustment to a new culture was overwhelming. I was terrified of failing.

I was about to quit and return to Brazil when a friend, Jane, introduced me to the Landmark Forum. During the program, I distinguished myself from many of the meanings I had created in life. I took responsibility for my actions, forgave myself and others, and cleaned up resentments and regrets with my parents, siblings, and past boyfriends. I was experiencing a new kind of power, freedom, and new confidence to continue in the graduate program.

I met Bill, my future husband, at Landmark in December of 2003. We both had the foundation of authenticity, integrity, and responsibility we gained from the Landmark programs. The first months of dating were magical, and we were engaged within a couple of months. We were married on my birthday the following year.

Soon, our relationship started not working. Fundamentally we were two different, strong-willed people. Bill wanted things to be his way, and

I didn't agree with many of his choices. We constantly pushed each other's buttons. We hated who we were in the relationship.

Divorce started to be part of our conversations, and we sought couples therapy where we pushed through some of our struggles. We welcomed our daughter Maya to the world as our tenth anniversary approached. Maya has been the greatest gift and has inspired my transformation and healing.

At the peak of COVID, with all activities online, Maya and I decided to go to Brazil for an unknown period. After four months at my mothers' house, I didn't want to go back home to the US, but staying wasn't a choice.

Bill and I had a critical conversation over the phone from Brazil when we decided we'd proceed with the divorce. I worked hard trying to make it work, fix myself, and accept Bill. And there was nothing else to fix or change.

I knew I needed to connect with Bill in order to disconnect. After Maya and I returned to the US, I started the process by making a list of all we needed to split: house, bills, furniture, phone, insurance, cars, money, bank accounts, wedding ring, name change, etc. One by one, we resolved them, and slowly we were detaching.

I joined a health program as I needed to be empowered and in charge of my eating. I also connected with my spiritual teachers, especially Rev. Michael Beckwith of Agape International, and created my prayer:

> *Love, divine beauty, and powerful presence that governs the universe. It's with profound gratitude that I thank you for everything that brought me to this day, location, and time on this planet. Take me to the places, people, beings, creatures, and nature that will give me the messages and will guide me to the fulfillment of my mission in this life. Guide and protect me. Whisper the messages in my ear, and send me dreams that would spark the actions I need to take.*

I was guided and introduced to incredible mentors and healers in the coming months. During a shamanic healing session with Dani Mansfield, I realized how my past incarnations impacted all I was experiencing. I could see how many life events and struggles were opportunities to heal the past.

As I completed the daily forgiveness prayer part of the How To Heal course, my connection with the divine and the spiritual realms started to expand. I prayed for forgiveness to all the spirits I have ever hurt and those who hurt me in this and previous lives. The feelings of shame, guilt, resentment, and regret were losing their grip on me.

I was guided by the spirits and my angels by countless synchronicities and miraculous manifestations. Spirits often spoke through young Maya. We were sitting on the backyard swings when Maya said: "I am bored of this house. Can we live in a different house?" That allowed me to include her in searching for a new home without mentioning the divorce.

Finding our new home was a miracle. After months of failed attempts to rent a house, I was exhausted and stopped looking. One morning, as I woke up around five am, I had the idea to take a quick look at Zillow.

There I found our new home: a beautiful, safe two-bedroom, two-bath home in a four-acre compound surrounded by nature, with a swimming pool, located six minutes from Bill's house and Maya's school. I could see the guidance of my angels up to that moment and that I had to go through the months of failures to be ready to get this amazing home!

Moving week was the most challenging. Making the decisions on what to take and what to leave was difficult. I wanted Bill's home to be functional and familiar for Maya. I was stressed and exhausted even before I started to move and pack. Thanks to the help of dear friends Marcio and Carlos, my new house quickly became a temple.

Windows surround our new home, and I can easily be connected with the sunrise, sunset, and the moon! During a clear night in November, I suddenly woke up at 3:30 am and could not go back to sleep. I got up and wondered: *Why is it so dark on a full moon?* As I walk outside, I see the lunar blood eclipse! I lit a fire and experienced the perfect alignment of the sun, earth, and moon, similar to the day of my birth! What a gift!

A community of new friends, mentors, and spiritual healers started to surround me. I had profound experiences with plant medicine which further revealed that the power I was seeking is within me. I started to be present to my own medicine, the ability to heal myself, and to connect with the spirits and other dimensions.

I experience my fears of rejection, abandonment, and death with surrender. I saw traumas from my childhood once hidden from my view. And as I allowed myself to feel the pain, guilt, shame, resentment, and anger, I also allowed myself to release and transform it into the most wondrous gift.

As the space of rebirth emerged, I was left with the opportunity to recreate myself. I now understand that taking care of my body and being responsible for my eating patterns is essential to my spiritual path and my power in life. I deeply understand now that my body temple is my access to experience love, pain, bliss, sorrow, joy, and grief. I can now love and honor my inner child and use my breathing to anchor and temper my emotions.

I could die today in peace, knowing that we are all connected, that Maya will be taken care of, and that we will always be one. As I explore new possibilities within new relationships and my work, I get that my foundation is loving myself and those around me, and expressing my truth.

My responsibility resides only in continuing to transform and heal myself. It's not my job to fix anyone nor to save the world, the poor, or the disabled. As I release myself, I release Bill. As I love myself, love emanates to those who surround me. As I shine my light, I allow others to do the same.

The legal divorce took only two-and-half months and was done entirely online. We were both transformed in the process, and we can now create a new relationship as Maya's parents with the foundation of love and partnership.

As I look in my eyes in the mirror, I am in love with the warrior I have become and am pleased with each step I've taken so far on this journey. I'm proud of my hair's white natural highlights, the scars of motherhood, the breasts that could not nurse, the stretch marks from Yo-Yo dieting, and the body shape I carry on my journey.

The divorce was a physically and emotionally exhausting process. Yet I never felt so spiritually supported by all my ancestors, my mother, siblings, friends, families, mentors, healers, and communities that stood by my side.

My broken heart is being softened, and it's now protected by a strong armor that has been forged by the love, light, and fire within me.

Today I embrace the declaration from the day of my birth: "I am beautiful, and I am perfect!"

Ana Palla is committed to making a difference and doing what it takes to heal and transform herself. She cherishes spending time with her daughter Maya. She loves photography, crystals, and exploring the integration of feminine and masculine energies. She seeks to interpret and assimilate the messages from nature's sacred elements through observation, sensation, and exploration. She is currently a faculty and staff at the University of Maryland and has worked in the field of accessibility, equity, and inclusion for over 25 years. Ana is expanding her activities aiming to impact and empower women worldwide.

Contact Ana at
https://www.linkedin.com/in/ana-palla/ or anapalla@yahoo.com.

Ana Palla
+1 (703) 599-0519

CHAPTER 6

TALE OF THE TWINFLAMES

Jenny Campanilla, ReConnective Way Practitioner

"And they lived happily ever after" is the ending most people want to experience in life. Books and movies have everyone believing that if you look hard enough, you'll find your soulmate, and everything will work out. If you dive in deeper, you'll learn that not only do you have multiple soulmates in your lifetime, but you also have someone called a twin flame.

At first, glance, marrying your twin flame seems like a better deal. You learn that you're one soul split between two physical bodies. They say that your souls have the same blueprint and that they're your perfect mirror. Supposedly, nobody is *more perfect* for you than your twin flame. What they do not tell you is how challenging and tumultuous it is. All the arguments that ensue while they show you your deepest insecurities, fears, and shadows. They don't tell you about all the pain that follows those arguments and the self-doubt you end up having. They allude to the fact that, at times, the confrontation between you and your twin flame is so intense it can sometimes lead to being catastrophic.

Most importantly, they don't tell you your twin flame does not have to be the person you marry. In fact, it doesn't have to be someone you're even romantically interested in. We are the Campanilla sisters and are here to shed the truth about being twin flames.

Growing up in a Catholic family, we were taught not to believe in witchcraft or otherworldly gods from the start. We believed that while angels and demons existed, there were no such things as ghosts or magic. Despite all of this, divination and the occult was something my sister and I always gravitated towards. It was one of the only subjects we liked that we had in common. While she played with blocks and painted, I liked to play with dolls and read. While she focused on school and astronomy, I had my imaginary friends to play with at home. I played the piano, and she played the guitar. We couldn't be more different from each other. However, when it came to fairies, ghosts, mermaids, and aliens, you couldn't tear us apart from each other. We would spend hours watching shows like *Ghost Whisperer,* where we got to watch Melinda Gordon speak to ghosts, or *Supernatural,* where Sam and Dean fought all things supernatural. While watching these shows, we never imagined we would grow up doing the same thing ourselves.

When we jumped back into our spiritual journey, Melissa and I both came out of relationships. While she was coming out of a long-term relationship, I was coming out of a fast-paced karmic one. On top of that, we were both going through a dark time and trying to find our path in this world. Melissa took a gap semester from college since she forgot to submit her deposit to secure her spot, and I was getting over breaking my foot and learning how to walk again. It was hard to be there for each other since we've always done things differently.

Our lives and the situations we found ourselves in always coincided, however, we always had different coping mechanisms. I buried my head in books and TV shows, while Melissa turned to YouTube. While going through her recommendations one day, she saw a video about how to work a pendulum. Out of curiosity, she tried it out on herself and was amazed when it worked instantly. After trying out a few questions on herself, she ran into my room to show me. Her discovery floored me. *If Melissa can do it, I can do it,* I thought to myself. I asked the pendulum a simple question and waited for it to move. I felt a hollow pit in my stomach when my necklace just kept spinning and spinning in circles. "Well, maybe you just have a few blockages you need to clear up," Melissa told me. She went on about how her higher self was helping her deliver the answers, and I had some spiritual work to do to connect to mine. Instead of letting that stop me, I devoted my time to reading up on chakras and their meanings.

Learning how to unblock them became my first priority. If I was going to dive into this, I wanted to do it the correct way. While learning all about them, I came to the conclusion that I needed to see a shaman. That way, I could start with a clean slate and have all my chakras open and aligned.

The first shaman I went to immediately mentioned my sister. She told me, "You're not on this journey alone." This made sense to me since Melissa was the one that started us down this road with her pendulum. She said, "This isn't your first lifetime together. There won't be any progress without the other." Taking that with a grain of salt, I tried to steer the shaman back to my journey to help me unblock my chakras.

As soon as we ended the session, I called Melissa straight away. "You need to book a session with this shaman so you can get your chakras unblocked." However, Melissa was in the middle of learning about numerology and birth charts.

"I'll book a session once I'm ready," she said.

With the newfound energy and my chakras unblocked, I went home to try the pendulum again. To my dismay, it still didn't work for me. I barged into Melissa's room. "Check if my charkas are still open!"

I had finished the session no more than 30 minutes prior. When she checked for me, I still had certain chakras blocked.

Interestingly, the chakras I had open were the ones blocked for Melissa, and vice versa. Wanting a distraction from the fact that the session was a bust, I asked Melissa, "Tell me more about birth charts."

"The charts are basically a road map for who you are," she explained. "I'm using this to understand more about who I am, so I don't feel so lost."

In doing this, we were able to learn more about each other and how some aspects she had in her birth chart directly correlated to mine. Amazed by all this, I kept asking her if she could read my birth chart. That way, I could maybe see why all this wasn't working for me.

"Why can't you do it yourself?" She said.

"Nothing about this is coming to me naturally, Melissa. Maybe this is your thing, and I'm just supposed to be your manager or something."

"Well, you're obviously not trying hard enough. If you want it done, do it yourself."

Melissa and I got into an explosive fight about all of this. It got to the point where we didn't speak to each other for weeks. We couldn't even be in the same room with each other. I felt like she was purposefully withholding from me, while she felt like I was trying to exploit her talents. I wasn't sure why she wouldn't just help me. We didn't realize that her denying me all of this was her way of helping me find my own path in this journey.

Desperately wanting to find a mentor in all of this, I went on Etsy and found someone to tell me about my spirit guide. After waiting a week for her reply, I finally learned about Troy. He was my older brother from a past life and turned into my spirit guide to help guide me through this life. "You're here to help and teach," he said. "You just have to believe in yourself and be open to receiving your gifts."

Towards the end of the message, he mentioned Melissa again. "Your paths are very interwoven. You need to work together on this."

Knowing I needed to tell Melissa about this, I ended our three-week-long silence and had her read the message from Troy. If anything, it left us both perplexed. How could he be so adamant that we were to work together in this lifetime when I still had no idea what I could do. I ended up purchasing another reading from the seller, and she proceeded to tell me how I was an extremely gifted healer. She said, "This is something you and your sister did in *all* of your lifetimes together."

I started to get annoyed that every time I tried to have a reading, Melissa was brought up. It didn't make any sense to me that my sister would be linked to the answer every time I asked a personal question. Coming to the conclusion that I needed more answers, I booked a session with Tiffany. Little did I know that this one session would change my and Melissa's world.

I didn't know what to expect. Although the psychic on Etsy told me I was extremely gifted, I still couldn't do anything that Melissa could do. While she could use the pendulum, read tarot, and was a natural at birth charts and numerology, I just had the seven chakras memorized. Yes, I had a name for my spirit guide, but it wasn't like I could communicate with him. I was still too scared to even sit in meditation. When I sat down with Tiffany, she asked, "What would you like to receive from the reading?"

"I want to know why I wasn't gifted and my sister is," I said.

She wasn't the only gifted one in my family. We have a few aunts, uncles, and cousins who are mediums, so in my mind, it wasn't fair that they all had spiritual gifts, and I was struggling so hard even to get the pendulum to move.

Tiffany chuckled, "I'm not even able to use the pendulum," she said. "When I try to use it, my energy always overpowers the outcome."

Starting to feel hopeful, since that was what happened to me, I went on about how I kept trying to do things my sister could do, but it didn't come naturally to me. She finally smiled and casually said, "Well, it's because you two are twin flames!"

My heart stalled at that, and I got goosebumps all over my body. *That wasn't possible. We were sisters, not two people about to fall in love with each other.* My session went on and I felt renewed and restored by the end of it. I felt like I was finally awakening from a deep slumber, and I could finally see the road between Melissa and me unfurl.

When I got home, I ran to her room and debriefed her on everything.

"But we're sisters, not lovers," she said.

"Yeah, I'm confused about that part too, but it makes sense!"

We sat there a while, comparing everything about how our lives mirrored each other. It was so eerily similar, down to the boys we dated. While I dated a Rick, she dated a Nick. We had a pair of boyfriends born on the same day and another pair whose birthdays were days apart. We both started wanting to go the med school route, then we decided that wasn't the path for us around the same time. All this was going on without the other knowing. With the similarities, we noticed a lot of opposites we had. While I was loud and an extrovert, she was quiet and introverted. I was confident, and she was self-conscious. The more we talked about it, the more we saw a seesaw pattern. There would be times in our lives when she would change and be the confident one, and I would be the self-conscious one. Knowing all this, we decided to try and apply it to our spiritual journey.

It turned out that even our gifts complemented each other. After a lot of practice, I could finally stand on my two feet. Communicating with Spirit soon came naturally to me and is something I now do on a daily basis. I found my calling in energy healing and animals. I soon found out that those so-called imaginary friends I had when I was younger were actually spirit guides that still help me to this day. I discovered I had an affinity towards communicating with animals and healing them both mentally and physically.

Where I tend to stray towards the metaphysical aspect, Melissa veered towards astrology and numerology and wanted to become a certified life coach. Instead of working with animals, she wanted to help be the transformative compass in people's lives. While I save lost animals at the animal rescue for which I work, she wants to help people who feel lost. Melissa wants to teach them to learn about themselves through the lens of love and light and realize they have the ability to rewrite their whole identity. She wants to show people how to heal past wounds and let go of trauma responses and anxiety while I use my energy healing to help clear up stagnant energy affecting your physical reality.

Just like all balanced things, there are of course, the challenging aspects of being twin flames. We both bring out the insecurities and the shadow side from one another and push each other to uncover uncomfortable truths. The confrontations with this can sometimes be so catastrophic that it leads to weeks of not speaking to each other. To get over these arguments, both have to face truths we don't want to face about ourselves. It forces us to pause and reflect and try to understand the other. When they use the term looking in the mirror, it also means seeing your flaws reflected back to you. Sometimes, Melissa and I don't even realize what those flaws are until it's brought up and shown to us by each other.

All in all, being twin flames is definitely a roller coaster. It's not the epic love romance that books and shows make it out to be. It takes a lot of effort to maintain harmony and balance. It's a lot of sleepless nights due to fights, sharp words, and uncomfortable truths. However, being twin flames also means unconditional love. It's the knowing that no matter what, you do have your other half there for you through the good and the bad. Our spiritual journey may have just started, but Melissa and I have been on this ride through multiple timelines and can't wait to pick up where we left off last lifetime.

As of February 2022, Melissa has enrolled in the Pause Life Coach Training Program, getting certified as a Trauma-Informed Life Coach, specializing in healing and self-development with a spiritual approach. This will help her carry out her true purpose and fulfill her mission here on Earth. You can stay updated on her spiritual journey by subscribing to her youtube channel, where she posts videos about spirituality, self-love, healing trauma, personal development, goal-reaching, and stepping into your highest self. Be sure to stay tuned for one-on-one coaching sessions, available January 2023! As for Jenny, she currently helps manage an animal rescue in Northern Virginia. While she helps save puppies and kittens, she is also practicing her craft in energy healing on both humans and animals. She also does animal communication for anyone who needs help understanding their pets. Jenny recently started practicing the ReConnective Way. She started this part of her journey thanks to Tiffany, who was the best mentor Jenny could have ever manifested. Jenny and Melissa plan to open their own Etsy shop called Anela Ascendant.

YOU ARE THE MEDICINE

CLAIMING THE EARTH-SHAKING MAGIC WITHIN YOU

Ellen Mathys, MPH, Shamanic Healer,
Evidential Medium, Spiritual Channel

My fingers tightly gripped my seatbelt as I peered out the window of the dusty Land Rover. Mere inches separated the treacherous mountain road from the ravine below. We sighed with relief when we finally spotted the remote village, a scattering of sunburned mud-brick buildings with corrugated metal roofs. Villagers in traditional white garments spilled out of the buildings to investigate the visitors. I stepped forward, introduced the team to the village leaders, and explained our mission: to learn whether people had enough food and figure out if food aid was needed. Twelve village residents gathered to talk with us. We sat knee-to-knee on a worn grass mat on the packed dirt.

I asked the usual assessment questions. "How much grain is in your granary? How many meals do you eat daily?" They replied grimly, their eyes boring into me. "We have nothing. The granaries are empty. Our children eat small bits of bread at nighttime. Adults eat only wild plants that we collect in the bush, which fill our stomachs but cause stomach cramping. If you don't bring food aid, we'll die." I froze, struggling to process the stark severity of their situation and figure out what to say next. The village was bleak—no livestock wandering around, no market tables loaded with crimson tomatoes and emerald-green leafy veggies. The air was thick with desperation. My intuition was screaming. *They are teetering on the brink—get help now!* As we rushed back to the capital to mobilize assistance to the village, I wondered, *Why does humanity experience so much suffering? What will it take to make that end? Is what we're doing here enough?*

My longing to work in Africa began when I was young. Perhaps my ancestors etched it into my bones. My great-aunt Emma devoted her life to teaching in schools for girls in pre-independence Kenya. Half a century later, during a college study abroad program in Kenya, I lived in a cozy dung hut, researching the traditional milk-and-blood diet of the Maasai. I am blessed to have spent time among pastoral communities, like the Maasai, the Somali, and the Wodaabe. I loved hearing the rhythmic shuffling of camel and cattle hooves on the dirt, seeing the splash of brightly hued fabrics against the earthen landscape, and smelling the cooking-fires at evening-time. A sense of homecoming in these places defies logical explanation for this white urban American woman.

Driven by a desire to return to Africa and be of service, I completed my Master's Degree in Public Health at Tulane University in New Orleans, specializing in International Nutrition and Food Security and Complex Emergency and Disaster Management. I peered at a world map, located the tiny country of Burundi in Central Africa, and accepted an internship there doing rural health surveys. Burundi was in the grip of civil conflict, so I traveled by military convoys, communicated via walkie-talkies, and trained in how to handle limb amputations from land mines and abduction by rebels.

Six months later, I accepted a job in neighboring Rwanda, a country still seized by aftershocks of the genocide that killed a million people less than three years earlier. Violence in the Rwandan genocide was intimate. It was neighbor against neighbor, priest against parishioner, and friend against friend. In both countries, the pain and grief from ethnic conflict were rarely spoken of in public. But I was an empath, able to feel people's unspoken emotions and sense the earthbound spirits that wandered the land because they were not yet in the light. It was overwhelming, so I subconsciously silenced my intuition. That helped somewhat. I became less aware consciously of people's pain, and I could get through each day.

But I didn't realize at the time that pain and sorrow, both my own and others', seeped into my bones and hardened, my guttural cries of grief not yet expressed.

I finished the work in Rwanda and sought solace in the company of friends in New Orleans, where I met my future husband Bob. Then I accepted my dream job as a Regional Food Security Advisor for East and Central Africa. With time the relationship with Bob grew serious, so I moved back to New Orleans and spent several years teaching food security and consulting with aid agencies in Africa. My soul especially lit up when I traveled to the Sahel, a flat sweep of grassy savannah stretching across Africa. The Sahel is a magical transition area where the Sahara in the north slowly gives way to lush forests and farmlands to the south.

Bob and I married and decided to start a family. Following an intuitive nudge towards international adoption, we joyfully adopted Sofia, a beautiful five-month-old girl from Ethiopia with sparkly eyes and natural effervescence. Parenting a daughter of Africa deepened my relationship with the continent and its people, as I honor her heritage and feel a connection to her birth family as my own. With time, we've learned to navigate the complexities of adoption, especially international and transracial adoption, with tenderness, respect for Sofia's experience, and humility. Parenting a black child also led me to address my internalized white supremacy and patriarchal thinking as a white westerner.

We moved to Atlanta so Bob could work at the US Centers for Disease Control and Prevention (CDC). My consulting work involved frequent long international trips. In time the truth became clear: I needed to put family first and stop the international travel for a while. That was gut-wrenching and disorienting, as my self-image was wrapped up in work. *Who am I if I am not doing this work? Am I abandoning the communities we're serving? Will I ever be able to do this work again?* I felt lost and desperately needed spiritual guidance, but my intuition had been suppressed and neglected for years. I needed a teacher who could help restore my inner connection to divine wisdom.

They say that when the student is ready, the teacher appears. I found wonderful training programs and spent years training in psychic development, shamanism and Reiki. Immersing in the intuitive arts was like dancing in the first rains after a long dry season. Spirit guides appeared in meditation, some familiar from childhood and others unfamiliar, to reassure me that the connection to the spirit world had never left; it just needed to be nurtured and developed. As my intuitive abilities grew, I began to see clients for psychic readings and shamanic energy healing. But even as I did that work, I still internalized a patriarchal devaluation of my own intuition. I felt severed into two separate people, a type-A high-performer ready to work 24/7/365 to reduce human suffering in Africa, and a shamanic healer who knew the path to sustainably reducing humanity's suffering was through reconnection with the soul. I had no idea how to integrate the two until a new teacher came along.

Elder Malidoma Somé, a Dagara Elder and shaman from Burkina Faso in the Sahel, taught in nearby North Carolina. I participated in three programs with Elder Malidoma: Indigenous African Spiritual Technologies, Cowrie Shell Divination, and Kontomble Divination. When Elder Malidoma taught, every word was delivered, heavy with medicine and shimmering with the wisdom of the ancients, directly to my bones. In that grace-filled healing circle, I was able to shed layers of defensiveness, toxic cultural programming, and pain and restore my relationship with the spirit world, nature, and my true self. I learned that Spirit and the ancestors send everyone who incarnates on earth with gifts and medicine that the world needs. I was finally beginning to see my own medicine fully.

Elder Malidoma taught Ancestralization, which involved honoring the ancestors and doing spiritual healing work with ancestors who needed healing. Although I had worked hard in therapy to process grief from working in war zones, I had done little to understand my own ancestral trauma. My ancestors hailed from Europe and the British Isles. My father's ancestors settled in rural Nebraska, scratching out a meager living farming land taken from Plains Indians in the mid-1800s. Many of my ancestors were by all accounts hard-working and kind. But unfortunately, my great-grandmother was notoriously cruel, controlling, and abusive to her husband, my great-grandfather, and her son, my grandfather. The pain and trauma were passed down from generation to generation, and my father's upbringing bore the scars. I grew up learning that some of my ancestors were terrible people, and I blamed them for any suffering that we were experiencing in my family. I resolved to disown, forget and rise above them. But just like the pain from Rwanda and Burundi, the pain passed down from the ancestors just seeped into the bones.

When Elder Malidoma invited us to honor our ancestors and connect with specific ancestors for healing, Spirit intuitively directed me to work with my father's abusive grandfather. He still needed healing in the spirit world. I protested. *"No! My ancestors don't deserve healing."* But I learned that our ancestors are souls who deserve gratitude for the gift of our lives. Even ancestors with the most hurtful legacies are likely to be wiser and kinder as souls than the villains that we might imagine them to be, and they may experience healing in the spirit world if we can offer them grace. When I began to communicate directly to my ancestors, I couldn't keep my pain locked away anymore. The floodgates of my grief and anger burst open, and I became so overwhelmed that when I got to my room, I collapsed to the floor and had a six-hour panic attack. When the sun rose, I shakily gathered my things and hit the highway, screaming and sobbing at the ancestors in a four-hour meltdown as I drove back to Atlanta.

To truly heal, sometimes we must fall apart to come back together again in a new way. Drawing on Elder Malidoma's teachings and other resources, I began a years-long process of healing my ancestral lineages, with the loving guidance and protection of guides and angels in the spirit world. I learned to establish energetic boundaries with spirits, the same way you do with living people. I finally voiced my hurt and anger at ancestors who had brought so much pain to the family while alive. But I also understood they had been hurt themselves. I took personal responsibility for how I held onto and expressed my pain, and I began to extend grace to the ancestors that allowed forgiveness and trust to blossom.

Spirit repeatedly sent evidence of the healing going on in the spirit world. My jaw dropped when a psychic reader, knowing nothing of my family history, said: "Your uncle is here, from several generations up on your father's side, from Nebraska. He says that he died a broken man, with sadness and heartache. He still felt that pain in the spirit world—many in the family did. But when you started seeing the light in the ancestors, they saw their own light, and now they are reignited." As my ancestors healed, they became my most enthusiastic supporters in the spirit world. They choreographed eye-popping coincidences, like having strangers approach me with information I needed and telling me exactly where to find long-lost things. Spirit encouraged me to share my story publicly, which I stubbornly resisted, but Spirit was insistent. In 2020, an associate producer from PBS's *Finding Your Roots* television show with Henry Louis Gates Jr., reached out to me because my father's lineage—the same lineage I was working so hard to heal, would be featured on the show. Then I learned of the chance to write my story for Sister Armor. I trust the divine choreography and welcome the grace that is meant to flow through it.

I once asked Spirit why we must go through hardship to come into our full selves, especially for those of us called to be healers or shamans. *I used to be a world traveler with a great job. My life was totally under control! Now here I am, wading through pain from the ancestors I worked hard to forget. Isn't there an easier way to become a healer? Why do we have to fall apart?* Spirit gently responded. *We could tell you what you need to know about human suffering, but it's not the same as living it. You must have the emotional experience of the wounding and healing from it before you can be fully present and compassionate with others in their wounding. When you go through difficulties, they're often designed to crack you open, make you soften and surrender, so you can learn who you truly are.* I responded, *so it's like that old saying,* "All things are broken; that's how the light gets in?" They corrected me tenderly. *No, all things are broken; that's how the light gets out. By tending to your own wounding, you discover who you really are, and you discover the places where your gifts and medicine are hidden. Then you can live your medicine authentically in the world.* Our medicine is not only our gifts and strengths but also our courage to lean into our woundedness and genuinely heal.

Feeling despair in the Ethiopian village years ago, I asked Spirit, *Why does humanity experience so much suffering? What will it take to make that end?* Spirit has spent the last two decades guiding me towards an answer. Humanity's journey of expansion arcs towards peace and oneness with the Divine. But the path to get there is messy by design. As souls, we choose to incarnate on Earth, knowing many of the difficulties that may lie ahead. It may seem easier to float in the heavenly realms, but if you're looking to grow and evolve as a soul, Earth has what you're looking for. Fear forces you to find your courage. Conflict fuels strength and self-knowledge. Harm invites you to forgive. When you feel broken, sometimes that is when the true light of your being begins to shine.

Many people feel disconnected from their souls, ancestors, and communities. It was not always this way; traditional societies tended to honor the gifts of all their members. The African word *Ubuntu* means "I am because we are" or "humanity towards others." I believe our humanity is tightly intertwined, like a sweetgrass braid. I spent two decades in the international aid field trying to ease suffering before realizing that crises are a natural expression of a world on fire. In shamanism, fire is power, initiation, and purification. It drives destruction, creation, and individual achievement. People need fire to grow, but it must be balanced with water, which soothes, nurtures, and heals. Energetically, our world is on fire, and there is not enough water to temper the fire. A world in balance would temper achievement and innovation with care for all of its members, even where it requires making uncomfortable compromises. So many people, despite their good intentions, focus on setting fire to perceived obstacles or challenges without realizing that without water, you simply fan the flames into an inferno.

I wasn't sure how to translate this shamanic wisdom into my work until one morning in 2018, my eyes suddenly snapped open, and the words *Greenlight! Now go do it!* hung in the air. I intuitively knew I had agreed with Spirit to do something big, but what? Over the next few days, Spirit told me to start my own shamanism training program. I hesitated; *who am I to teach shamanism?* Spirit was loving but firm. *Your medicine is building sacred healing communities and leading rituals, so people can reconnect with their souls and discover their own medicine. You will do this around the world. Your family history, international work, and spiritual journey have prepared you for this. Are you ready to fully live your medicine?*

I took a deep breath, planted my feet firmly on the Earth, and said, "Yes." I established Wild Sage Healing Arts and developed a shamanic program called MoonRise. MoonRise participants learn many ancient spiritual and shamanic techniques, including energy healing on people and animals, mediumship, and psychopomp (leading earthbound spirits into the light). They reconnect with their ancestors and spirit guides. They discover their medicine, release old programming, heal from trauma, and realign their lives to support their purpose. The fire in their souls is fully ignited but balanced with the soothing waters of non-judgmental support and genuine healing. Angels, star beings, ancestors, and other spiritual beings encircle us to hold ritual space, provide unwavering support and join in our celebrations.

To support intuitive youth who struggle with their gifts, I launched a program called Level Up. Level Up provides youth with support and training, so they can use their psychic gifts correctly and safely in a community that sees and values them for who they are. I see clients for quantum energy healing, psychic readings, hypnotherapy, and I channel many-dimensional light beings. I'm developing a quantum healing modality that connects people with their higher selves and Spirit, restores integration across the soul and its incarnations, and promotes physical healing. And I embrace my deep connection to Africa, that powerful continent where I have lived so many past lives and which continually beckons me to return.

People express their medicine in countless ways. Your medicine may express in teaching, construction, parenting, math, health care, the arts, or other fabulous forms. When we live our medicine authentically, we raise our frequency and beam that frequency out into the universe. By shining our light, we encourage others to heal and shine their light. As more people anchor into and live in their authenticity, we build an energetic bridge between the world as it is now and the world that's being created. Physical actions and programs that reduce suffering are essential and important. But it is our genuine healing and reconnection with the divine in ourselves and each other that will finally balance humanity's water and fire, end suffering, and bring peace. We must only answer that question from Spirit, posed with love and unwavering support, *Are you ready to fully live your medicine?*

Dedicated to Elder Malidoma Somé, Burkina Faso, Africa (1956-2021).

Ellen Mathys, MPH, is the Director of Wild Sage Healing Arts in Atlanta. She is a gifted shaman, quantum healer, evidential medium, spiritual channel, cowrie shell diviner, and creator of healing communities. She founded a world-changing shamanic training program called MoonRise, which she co-teaches with Kimmy Yon and Roxanne Lowery. MoonRise teaches ancient and powerful shamanic techniques, builds a sacred and supportive community, and helps participants discover and live their medicine. Ellen also teaches Level Up with Meggan Huntington, which teaches young folks to embrace and use their intuitive gifts. A skilled and meticulous evidential medium, Ellen connects people with their spirit guides and loved ones across the veil. She lovingly guides clients back to joy and wholeness with quantum hypnotherapy and healing (including past life regression and Arcturian healing), shamanic energy healing, Reiki, and evidence-based mediumship. She also channels many-dimensional light beings who are helping guide humanity's ascension.

Ellen spent 20 years working as an International Food Security and Early Warning and Response Specialist with international humanitarian and development agencies. She has worked in almost 30 countries in Africa, Central America, and the Caribbean, including many conflict-affected, displaced, and refugee populations. In the US, she has provided energy healing to incarcerated women, hospice patients, and horses that provide equine-assisted therapy to children. She adores spending time with her wonderful husband Bob and their phenomenal daughter Sofia. When not working, Ellen can often be found, muddy and deliriously happy, in the garden.

Connect with Ellen:

On her website: https://wildsagehealingarts.com

On Instagram: https://www.instagram.com/wildsagehealing

Email: ellen@wildsagehealingarts.com

CHAPTER 8

A JOURNEY
OF REMEMBERING

AWAKENING TO MY
ANCESTRAL CALLING

sekayi anika

"You have Stage IV endometriosis."

I focused on the stoic face of the surgeon as I lay in the hospital bed. I had just undergone laparoscopic surgery to remove an endometrioma cyst from my right ovary.

"I did what I could to clean it out. Only your left fallopian tube is working, and for the next six months, you can try to get pregnant. I'll see you in a year to remove your uterus."

"Okay, thanks," I managed to get out, still foggy from the anesthesia. I rested my head on the pillow and closed my eyes. A part of me was angry at his lack of bedside manner, but I realized my anger wasn't with him. It was with the reality of my situation: the fertility treatments I planned to begin afterward may not work.

Six months passed quickly, and with each excruciating menstrual cycle that arrived, the hopes of getting pregnant faded. A year and one month later, I scheduled a hysterectomy.

"How ya feelin'?"

I blinked to find the doctor standing at my bedside. He was a tall man with salt and pepper hair and kind eyes. I gave him a small smile and nodded my head. I was in pain.

"The endometriosis spread over all of your organs, and I needed to remove your appendix. We thought you'd need a blood transfusion because you wouldn't stop bleeding."

He handed me photos. It looked like everything was trapped under layers of silk webbing. All I could think of was me in an episode of ER with my stomach cut open and bleeding out. Thankfully, this wasn't television, and I made it home after a few nights in the hospital.

Having a total hysterectomy meant at a month shy of my 40th birthday, I was immediately thrust into menopause. I opted not to have hormone replacement therapy but tough it out on my own. I thought the night sweats alone would take me out, but there was also the lack of focus, energy, and the oh so pleasurable mood swings.

Sitting around for six weeks to heal allowed me lots of time to be still and think.

But my focus wasn't clear, and my thoughts were all over the place. There was one voice I began to hear asking:

Who are you? What are you? What are you doing? What have you done?

Nothing felt right. The brown sofa I laid across, the brown rug, brown curtains, brown wood trim—all of it felt drab. I knew this feeling: it was the beginning of a coming undone. Depression.

Depression hit me the hardest in college and every winter since I lived through the blues, looking for it and embracing it each time it came around. In this stillness, I could feel the immense pain from the surgery and something new—an emptiness.

Imagine you're in an overcrowded elevator pressed shoulder to shoulder. The bell rings, doors open, and a few people exit. You relax your shoulders; a few more people exit at the next floor. You breathe deeply. Again, the doors open, and the last people exit. That "emptiness" now allows you to have space to spread out, move around, breathe deeply and get comfortable.

That is the emptiness I felt. Space that was made inside. Something was removed from inside, and now there was space.

This space, however, made me uncomfortable, and I didn't want to be there. I felt guilty for needing help doing simple things. I felt like a slacker laying around all day. I began to press myself to get up and get moving. I walked around the block once a day until I returned to work after four weeks. I couldn't keep it up, though. I found myself sitting in my car longer each day, gathering the strength to put on a happy face. The voice within kept asking:

Who are you? What are you? What are you doing? What have you done?

I was born into a Christian family but wanted to explore something new. I found a nearby yoga and meditation studio run by a small-statured powerhouse of love and wisdom.

Uncomfortably, I sat cross-legged in a room facing a wall with strung lights behind a wall tapestry illuminating the design of a beautiful tree. My eyes were closed, as instructed, but I kept peeking to see if I was doing it "right."

"Hold your back straight and imagine your spine as a tube. As you inhale, imagine the breath coming down from the heavens, through the crown of your head, and down your spine."

I felt it travel down my spine.

"On your exhale, imagine the breath traveling back up your spine, out from the crown of your head, and back up to the heavens."

I felt it reverse up my spine.

"As you inhale and exhale each breath, you are breathing with God."

It was at that moment—after growing up in a Baptist church, being a minister in a Pentecostal church, earning a master's degree from Seminary in Christian counseling—that I felt God for the first time.

I wept quietly to myself as we sat in stillness.

Who are you? What are you? What are you doing? What have you done?

There was a woman nearby who offered Reiki sessions. Turquoise, green, and peacocks were the office theme. Her smile was huge, her southern accent was thick, and her random F-bombs made me chuckle. Not knowing what to expect, I lay on the table and watched as her hands hovered over my body. Once she reached my pelvic area—my now empty womb space—I began to feel the same stirring within me that I felt in the yoga studio. I closed my eyes and held my breath.

"You can release it," she said.

I began to wail deeply as she moved her hands all around me. I began speaking in tongues. I never experienced this "evidence of salvation" outside of a church setting, but it all came pouring out of me. Something shifted. I didn't know what and couldn't describe it, but something was different.

That Reiki experience, along with my new meditation practice, expanded my understanding of God. I was able to connect myself to that source of energy without any separation, need to be reconnected, need to be saved, or need to be reconciled. I went through her training and was attuned to all levels of Reiki. I completed the certification to provide this energy healing to others. I knew what opened for me, and I wanted to help it open for others.

Who are you? What are you? What are you doing?

I tapped into something I never knew or experienced before. When I was a kid, I was a tomboy who loved the outdoors, inspecting bugs, and bird watching. But this yearning for nature was something different. I would make my way out to a local creek early in the mornings before the joggers and dog walkers came so I could have time alone to pray, cuss and cry. I sat in silence most of the time and allowed the breeze and swaying tree leaves to give me songs and messages. I let the sounds of the flowing water soothe and strengthen me. I understood that I was connecting to that same energy source and became aware that I could find all I needed here. I can find a place of belonging, a place of security, a place of deep peace and tremendous love. Whenever I found times challenging, and I could not manage my humanness—or menopause—on my own, I made my way there to replenish and remember that connection.

Who are you? What are you? What are you doing?

One quiet morning while sitting on a huge rock with my bare feet in the cool waters, I came to realize that the one incessantly asking me, *"Who are you?"* was me—my divine self.

She had been trapped underneath the layers of endometriosis and years of self-neglect, going along to get along as a people pleaser, living in fear and doubt, and low self-worth. Once the uterus, ovaries, fallopian tubes, appendix, and silk layers of endometriosis were removed, there was more space. She could relax her shoulders, spread out, and get comfortable.

She looked out from within, saw that she was forgotten, and began to wonder:

Who are you? What are you? What are you doing? OMG! What have you done?

She then began her journey forward. No more hiding. No more being stifled. She was no longer trapped. She had space to move and wanted to be seen and heard. She was not stopping and was ready to help me remember and return to myself. The time had come.

A random email about African spirituality arrived in my inbox with a link to a podcast. A Sangoma priestess was interviewing a man. Her voice ignited that same stirring within me, and, again, I began speaking in tongues. I followed the link to her website and saw she offered divinations. I had tarot card readings before but never a divination.

Book the divination.

When the video connected, I saw she wore a beaded wig covering her face. Her voice was smooth and steady as she explained everything that would happen before we started.

"Blow into this shell."

I leaned into the computer screen and blew. For the next 45 minutes, my hand moved feverishly, taking notes as she told me all about myself and my lineages. She spoke of my father's side, whose energy around negative domestic activities needed clearing. She spoke of deep pain and sadness on my mother's side that needed resolution. She told me all about my spiritual imbalance and a need for discipline and ritual. She told me of fiery warrior and water ancestral spirits working to protect me and wanting to connect with me. She spoke of the urgency in connecting with these ancestors to assist me with my purpose, focus, and direction. The divination follow-up was to do ancestral cleansings and blessings if I felt so-called.

Do it.

I scheduled time for the follow-up sessions. This was my first time doing any type of ritual or spiritual bath. I shopped at two local metaphysical stores I began to frequent regularly to gather the rainbow colors of candles needed along with the required herbs. For seven days, I witnessed my senses gradually attune. It was as if I was Pig-Pen, and the cloud of energies circling me was clearing. I felt lighter and highly sensitive to people and energies around me. I also began to clearly see what was happening in my life.

I was asked to report my dreams and kept a small recorder next to my bed so they wouldn't escape me once my eyes opened each morning. Doing this reminded me of the dreams I had as a child. A recurring one was with me standing at the top of the stairs at my grandparents' house. Freely I flew down the steps, through the living room, above the plastic-covered sofa, through the dining room, into the kitchen, and back up the stairs. Being shown the meanings of my dreams during these follow-up sessions reminded me of the life that happens in the dream state and how the ancestors choose to show themselves, deliver messages and give instructions and guidance.

During one call, the priestess gave instructions on what to do while she drummed. The movement in sync with the rhythm of the drums: Boom bap! Boom boom boom boom boom! Boom bap! took me into a deep state of meditation. I found myself wet in a river of water. I was in the center of a circle of women wearing white ruffled skirts, white shirts, and white cloth wrapped around their heads. They spoke inaudible words of support and encouragement. I felt their love and strength.

Who are you? What are you? What are you doing? What have you done?

I stayed in touch with this priestess, and she invited me to a retreat in California. It was a beautiful and peaceful space. I had sat in many spiritual and metaphysical circles where I never felt like I belonged. However, this group of five gathered on the mountain felt like family. I never felt like I needed to guard, protect, question, or doubt myself. The rituals and ceremonies were foreign to me, but my spirit felt at home. I felt free. The drums played during one of the last ceremonies, and we sang beautiful songs. The priestess came over to me, I put my face to the ground, and the loudest and strongest sound erupted from the pit of my belly. When it stopped, I sat leaning against the wall, and a piece of red, black, and white fabric hanging across from me drew my attention. In the center was the head of a lion. I knew, at that moment, that this was where I was supposed to be.

Who are you? What are you doing? Where are you going?

Another invitation from the priestess led me to a spiritual temple in Baltimore. A few of us gathered for a weekend with an opportunity to meet her teacher and shadow a student who was currently in the process of her spiritual training. There were moments of laughter and great wisdom shared by the teacher, but the shadowing of the student was *hard*. I was mentally, emotionally, and physically exhausted. Near the end of the weekend, the teacher says, "It's obvious that you have a calling. What are you going to do?"

There is that question again.

The weekend revealed that my spirit felt at home the moment I entered the door. I belonged there. My spirit wanted to be there. I understood that I was not speaking in tongues, but my ancestors spoke through me. I knew all I was searching for in different circles was right here in this temple and with this teacher. And although everything up until that point gave me tremendous clarity on what the answer should have been to her question, an old familiar friend—fear—reemerged and responded for me:

"I'm too old. My body is not capable of doing this. What about my husband? I don't know where I'll get the money. I'm already doing healing work. I can keep taking classes with the priestess to learn all I need to know. Look at me. I don't think I can do this."

She simply says, "Okay," and leaves it at that. The ride to the airport was full of laughter and singing.

After that weekend, I had no plans to do anything else, but my ancestors wouldn't let up. That urgency to connect with them was felt and seen in the meanings of the dreams I recalled. When I gave Reiki sessions, they showed up to direct and guide me. When I heard *"blow in her stomach,"* I blew. I had no idea what or why, but I did whatever I heard. I knew that I needed something more and was being asked to do something more. In all this unfolding, I added a tagline to the name of my Reiki business: "restoring awareness of the divinity within." That's what they're asking me to do.

Who are you? What are you doing? Where are you going?

I emailed the priestess telling her I would answer the call, and two weeks later, my life turned upside down–or rather–right-side up.

"I think we need to split and go our separate ways," I said.

"So, you want a divorce?" he asked.

"Yes."

Each day, I looked guilt in the face and did not back down. This time I couldn't ignore my need to heal myself properly. I needed to stand firm in my decision and my truth. I moved to North Carolina and grieved the loss of the life I had just two months ago. It was hard, but I had a fresh start. Space was created, and this time it wasn't uncomfortable.

Who are you? What are you doing? Where are you going?

At the start of the global pandemic, I began my spiritual training to become a traditional African healer of the Sangoma tradition out of South Africa.

This is an individual journey back to self. One where there is a need to forget all that I knew to remember all of who I am—to go beyond labels, patterns of thoughts, and negative ways of being to reach the place that has no form. And to rediscover, remember, and reacquaint me to myself there. That place, for me, is divine love.

In remembering love for and to myself, things begin to align. I see myself from that place of love, and the way I look in the mirror has changed. I see deeper and with different eyes. I experience new things and welcome new opportunities simply because they're afforded to me. I don't have to seek them out, as I'm now aligned with all the goodness and sweetness that life has for me. I deserve them. And I'm the happiest I've ever been.

Who are you? What are you doing?

I am a divine being created in love. I am a child of the water, fire, wind, and earth. I am the granddaughter of greatness. I am chosen to carry the medicine of my ancestors for healing myself, my family, and my community. I am an embodiment of and named after the one who has called me. I am Moloi waYah Ngoba.

Now, who are you?

sekayi anika (meaning laughter and goodness) loves a good hearty laugh and surrounds herself with goodness—family, friends, and anyplace outdoors where she can connect with the earth, fire, air, and water.

sekayi anika is a serial crafter willing to try anything that looks fun at least once! A manifestation of the divine creator, she loves using her hands to make and build. Embodying that creative spirit brings her great joy—along with a handy power tool! In the flow of creativity, she remembered that she was a divine creator who had forgotten that it's okay to color outside the lines. And it was outside the conditioned lines of her life where she began her journey of healing and transformation.

sekayi anika found herself with moments of inspiration and sudden urges to write whatever thoughts, feelings, and emotions surfaced for release. In sharing her writing, she connected with others going through similar experiences. At the nudging of her older sister, Yolanda, sekayi anika self-published her first book *#imnowriter: a compilation of words+pics.* These writings speak of her moments of remembrance, surrender, and transformation. It also includes journal pages to reflect as you step across the lines and into your journey of healing and transformation.

Given the spiritual name Moloi waYah Ngoba, she is completing her training to become a Sangoma priestess. Her connection to her ancestors has given her life greater clarity, direction, purpose, and joy. As a bridge of love, her assignment is to embolden you to color outside the lines of your life and walk alongside you as you remember and revive the beautifully divine creation you are.

Connect with sekayi anika (Moloi waYah Ngoba):

On Instagram: https://www.instagram.com/sekayianika

CHAPTER 9

LIVING AN ESSENTIAL LIFE

STEPPING INTO YOUR NATURAL SELF

Mary Blanchard

Everyone is sharing hugs and kisses. I can barely hear what's said because there's so much chatter and loud pats on backs. People are smiling, laughing, and talking over each other while we kids line up, hands in our pockets, not knowing what to do. As I look out the front door, the lawn is dotted with red spots, the crabapples calling us out to play. But we silently stand there waiting to endure our hugs before we're released from the grownups.

Finally, the adults are done greeting each other, and move on to the kids. I accept a hug and then hear, "You'd be so pretty if you lost weight." I feel my neck turning red. I want to disappear. I shrink as much as I can. I look for places to hide. *Will they notice if I run away? I wish my bike had a basket, but I don't need to take much. I want to scream! Why do I always get singled out?* I pretend I'm invisible, and I don't exist. *When will this visit end?*

I've been told before, "I could be pretty if," but at this moment, I'm surrounded by family and friends. *I was looking forward to playing with all the kids, but now I'll be laughed at and made fun of. Why does everything get ruined?*

I constantly heard messages that I wasn't good enough, and didn't measure up. Every feeling I expressed I was told, "You're being overly dramatic." *Even my feelings are wrong?*

I don't want to go to bed. Nights stretch like taffy with thoughts of how I don't fit in sticking all over me. I'm crushed hearing the dreaded words, "Go to bed, and we'll tuck you in when we come up." I sulk my way up the steps, turn left into my bedroom and close the door. Walking straight up to my bed, I pull the pillow and blanket off and plop them on the floor. I flop down, arms folded, and rest my chin on my hands to wait. I have the perfect view under the crack of the door to see when they come upstairs.

I lay there and pray my parents won't forget me. I hold my hands in prayer and beg God, "Let me say too, I want to be the one to say, I love you too." I plead with God: *Please let them say they love me. They need to say it first, so I know I matter.*

I was scared there was something wrong with me. I believed the hurtful words, consumed and lived into them. I assumed them as fact and made up my own story of what they meant: I wasn't good enough; I didn't measure up; I was unlovable. I wore the negativity like a coat, layers of miles-thick wool to protect me. If I could keep everyone away, I'd be safe.

After 25 years of protecting myself—building walls and avoiding feelings—I begin to unravel. One night, as I get ready for bed, I look into the mirror and hear a voice say, *I don't like you.* I looked around the room. The voice was loud, it couldn't have just been in my head. Looking at myself, I know it's me. I stand there, leaning forward, hands on my hips, staring myself down, daring it to speak again. In the silence, I start to cry, softly at first, and then as the feelings wash over me, my body rocks with the heaviness of my sobs. I stand there bawling until my back aches, and I think I'm going to collapse. I drag myself to the bed and fall asleep under the weight of a thick sadness.

CREATING A SAFE SPACE

After this cracking open I begin to process and heal. I'm watching a PBS special, and during a fundraising break, Wayne Dyer comes on. Seeing and hearing him fills my body with peacefulness. I feel calm, protected, and seen. As he speaks, his right arm circles; it's hypnotic. I keep staring at him, and the TV fades away, it's only the two of us in the room, and he's talking directly to me. "The wake is nothing more than the trail that is left behind, and it has no power in the present. It's the present moment energy that is driving the boat. The wake does not and cannot drive the boat." I'm not exactly sure what the words mean yet, but I know they are powerful.

I start listening to Wayne Dyer's CDs in my car. Whenever I feel like I'm going to disappear, I get in my car, pop in one of his CDs, and drive over every country back road I can find. I drive through pouring rain on sunny days; whenever the mood hits. I drive up and down hills and listen until my breathing returns to normal and I can pull myself up on the lifeline he throws down to me. I feel the impact of his words and think they're fixing me. It's one step towards recovering myself. It creates a safe space to pause and pull myself out of the darkness.

I thought all there was to life was going down a hole and then finding ways to pull myself out. It was a YoYo routine I did for years, and each time I made it back out, I thought I was fixed.

PROCESSING

After so much time dangling on the YoYo, I was frayed. I wanted more, and gave myself the gift of working with a life coach. I spent my life and energy on avoiding my feelings, wishing away my experiences, and making up my own stories to somehow justify that I deserved them.

I'm an empath. I feel very deeply, and I cry easily at anything emotional. However, I started to see that I stopped myself from feeling. I disassociate myself from situations so I won't feel. I became the consummate avoider. On one of my first calls with the life coach, she said, "You may become a master crier." And I thought: *That's okay, I'll pass. I'm not going down that road. Dang! Here I am, still avoiding.* I spent my life trying to hide and disappear. I don't know how to open up and be vulnerable. The fear feels like it will swallow me up.

Patty has a phrase that still resonates with me. "All you have to do in life is show up, be present, be authentically you." *That sounds easy. Isn't there more to it? I'm pretty sure I already do that.* Oh, I had a long way to go! I had no idea who I was, and I didn't know that I didn't know who I was.

The next time I talked with a friend and told them how good everything was, I heard: *Lies! You're being fake. Why are you pretending everything is rosy when all you want to do is cry?* It shook me to realize that not only am I not present, but I'm also not being my authentic self, and I'm not most of the time. I spend days crying my way into work and crying my way back home. I shed enough tears to flood Route 66 during my three hours of driving back and forth each day. *I can't do this; it's too hard. I don't know if I can figure it out.*

And then it hits me. I caught myself in the act! I saw myself not being present, and I saw myself not being authentic. If I can see it, then I can change it. I get to choose a different path, response, reaction, whatever it is. If I can pause in that gap, I can show up. It created an awareness that kept peeking in like rays of hope, and I couldn't stop seeing it.

Now I can step in and stop being on autopilot. To regain control of my feelings, if I'm hurt or upset, I ask myself: *What do I really know about this situation, and what have I made up?* I tried having all the conversations in my head, thinking out the different possible scenarios, but the reality is that most of the time, I don't have enough information to make a judgment, so I need to stop spinning my wheels. Sitting with the not knowing is uncomfortable, but it doesn't drive me as crazy as making up my own story to keep beating myself up with. It's a practice and sometimes I forget, but eventually it comes to me, and I pause to ask myself, what are the facts I know for sure? I then step back into myself and figure it out or seek out more information.

ACCEPTANCE

I'm reclaiming the beach. Walking on the beach used to make my thoughts race with anxiety. *Do I fit on the beach? Will people think I'm too fat or ugly? Will people laugh at me?* Now, I know I belong as I press my feet into the sand. My shoulders soften as my stride matches the rhythm of the sea.

The sand is glistening, and as I pause to watch the water, I notice the ocean tosses out beautiful shells as if they're nothing. People walk by, paying them no attention. I want to stop them and say, "Look at them; each is a gem. They shine on the sand. Water runs over them again and again, smoothing out their rough edges." I want to collect each one of them and shower them with love and attention.

I know I can't save them all, so I stand over them and watch and whisper, "You're beautiful, and you're loved. You make the beach sparkle."

I know I'm saying this as much to myself as I'm saying it to the shells. *How ironic, I'm no longer just a shell of myself.* Walking along the beach, I'm part of royalty. The shells and stones are cheering me on. *You're one of us, you're beautiful, and you're seen.*

Now looking at the beach, my former anxiety of not being good enough is gone. I feel relaxed and see all of the natural beauty. The birds walk along the beach, leaving behind their webbed feet marks or standing looking for food. The flow of the tide is constant, and I watch it roll in and out. The waves, the foam: every time it's different. I see the sand, the tracks that people, cars, and birds make, the water line that feeds in and out, the shadows we all cast on it. What a difference a lifetime makes. I've stepped into my body, it's served me well, and I'm not hiding.

SUPPORT

It started with one drop. When I walked into the room, I didn't know that my life was about to bloom. It was a simple invite from a friend, and I'm that friend who always shows up. It doesn't matter what's going on; I'm interested. Count me in. My friend could have mentioned essential oils. I don't remember. It wouldn't have resonated with me at the time because I didn't know what they were. One drop, that's all it took to explode my world.

We sat on folded chairs with our purses sitting on the floor. A bottle of peppermint oil is handed to me. "Put a drop in the palm of your hand, then put your thumb into it and press it on the roof of your mouth," she says and as I do it, "Now inhale." My eyes pop wide! *I think we just achieved world peace,* and my chest opens up. *What is this?* I have clarity. I'm alert, alive, and invigorated. Rachel sees my eyes and laughs. "I think Mary just had an orgasm," she says as she looks around the room to make sure no one is offended by her words. Everyone laughs. But at that moment, everything aligned for me.

I keep inhaling the cooling sensation and put my palm to my nose for that sweet freshness. *My mom needs to add this to her brownies. They would change lives!* I didn't know what they were talking about up to that point, but I'm awake now. The room smells nice because there are oils in a diffuser, but I have candles that can do that. No, this is much more than the aroma. I feel different. Putting that drop of peppermint oil in my mouth shook my world. This is a seismic shift. I've never experienced anything like it before. This is purity!

Each bottle of oil I smell transports me to the farm where it was harvested. I would swear I'm standing in the field with the farmers. I love how the scents of plants are their internal protection system. With pure essential oils on hand, I can provide myself the support I need when I need it, instead of waiting. My essential oil books are stacked next to my chair so I can read about the compounds of different oils. I imagine my chemistry teacher smiling as I have fun combining different blends.

Most days, I felt a heaviness leaving home, and I pushed my way through it. My heart raced, and my body was in knots. I didn't know there was a change happening. Until one day, as I walk to my car, I realize I can't remember the last time I felt that heaviness. Instead, I hear music blaring from a car passing by, and I want to dance. I sit in my car, turn on the music and let my body move.

The oils are one way I bring nature into my home. There are many tools I've picked up to fix myself throughout the years, but it wasn't until I discovered pure essential oils that I fully stepped into myself and became aware. I didn't need fixing. I was never broken.

Walking with nature is my temple to bring everything together in sweet harmony. I start by going to my essential oils to see what calls out to me. I inhale deeply and apply the oils, creating the mindset for my walk. My mind slows down and lets my soul catch up. As I step on the earth, I feel the connection. The woods are my feast.

Nature brings me present, and I can see all the details. At first, it feels like I'm walking in slow motion taking it all in, but it's my soul expanding to fill all my senses. Everything goes silent as I walk in awe of the beauty. Each twist of a tree or patch of moss makes my curiosity soar and connect deeper into myself. *I was once as twisted as that tree, trying to mold myself into what others thought of me.*

I walk, and listen. The birds chirp out their tunes over and over like a love poem they know by heart. *It is what I make it.* Every walk is different. It's all one big kaleidoscope that keeps on turning. I have to keep tuning in to see what's there because no one else has my view. *Everything I need shows up when I show up.* These are my roots, and they go deep, but they're also what allows me to grow strong. You can be told you're not good enough and still step forward and shine.

"Every minus is half of a plus, waiting for a stroke of vertical awareness." - Alan Cohen

Mary Blanchard wants everyone to know you're seen, and you matter. Your story is what the world needs to heal. You, exactly as you are, is what the world needs you to be. In sharing your story, others can accept and step into their own. In sharing your story, you create your own stroke of vertical awareness. Her mission is to create a safe space for everyone to shed their shame and walk into their light.

Mary is a wellness advocate with doTERRA and is passionate about sharing pure essential oils to support and uplift you. Whether you would like to join a group class or have a one-on-one consultation, Mary can guide you on your path with natural solutions. With more than thirty years of experience in the hospitality industry, she leads with a heart for service.

Wabi-sabi philosophy teaches us that beauty is found in imperfection. Cracks are filled with gold, so they shine and are celebrated. When was the last time you were celebrated? Mary would like to honor you and your journey to help you discover what makes your heart sing and your soul dance.

Let's get together and connect. To find out more about Mary, visit her website at www.naturallymb.com to schedule a free 20-minute essential oil consultation and read more of her writing.

CHAPTER 10

UNWIND

LOVE'S INTERVENTION OF A TIGHTLY WOUND SOUL

Mary Lloyd

"What are you going to do?" The question sounded like it was coming from another room. Erik gently asked again, "What are you going to do in retirement?" As I sat motionless, staring at the floor, it took a minute for me to respond, "Huh?" Right after Erik became my boss, I promised him that he would be the first to know if I ever decided to leave my position. Deep down, I hoped this conversation was enough to fulfill that promise. On the other hand, my soul wanted to be anywhere other than this conversation.

"With your new freedom from work, what are you going to fill your time with?" Erik continued to sprinkle polite questions to break up the long periods of awkward silence in this one-sided conversation. "Any fun hobbies?" My eyes instinctively shot an indignant glare at him before quickly returning to staring at the floor. "What about any fun travel plans?"

As I sat on the other side of Erik's desk fighting the lump in my throat, praying he couldn't see me trembling, tears started to stream down my face faster than the words came out of my mouth. "I don't know," came out so hushed I'm not sure I actually said it out loud.

He continued, "Retirement is a big achievement in a person's life. Something to celebrate."

With my eyes still locked on the floor, I forced out, "I don't know," just over the sounds of my quiet sobs.

"Don't worry; you'll have time to figure it out. You've put in your time here, much more than most. I'm in awe of all you've done, even without the support you should have had over the years. I want to make sure your remaining time is full of the fun parts of the job. You deserve it."

With tears freely flowing, I gathered enough strength to voice the pain of my decision. I fought to control my breath as my voice quivered. "I just don't want anybody else to have to go through what I've gone through. I mean, no one should have to go through that level of shit to do what they love."

Erik sat quietly. I took a few breaths to strengthen my voice. "I just can't do it anymore. I can't. There's so much more that can be done better. That should be done better. To get staff what they need to do their jobs. To help make better decisions for the resource."

For the first time in our conversation, I looked at Erik. My tears fell unchecked as I slowly shook my head and, with a plaintive voice, said, "I… I can't anymore. I want to. But I just can't." Before Erik could react, I don't know why but I bolted out of his office and into mine.

The walls shook as my office door slammed shut. I stood there behind the door for a moment, trembling, openly sobbing, and ashamed at my decision as I tried to process what to do next.

Ding. Ding. Fifty-three new emails in my inbox since I left to talk to Erik.

Ding. Ding. Ding. *Fifty-six! They fucking never stop.* Ding. Ding. *Brringg, brringg.* Ding. The constant bombardment of new emails and incoming phone calls snapped me into the robot I knew all too well. It was my tried-and-true survival mode.

Okay, you've got to pull yourself together. Just sit down, read a few emails, and get back in the game. I took a deep breath and sat down in my chair while skimming email subject lines.

Pffumph! Crack. *Fucking piece of a shit chair!* My years-long love-hate relationship with my hand-me-down office chair was complicated, to say the least. Crack. Crack. Clunk. "Shit!" Thud.

I don't know which happened first, me hitting the floor or the ugly crying. Sprawled out on my office floor, I was shattered. With each sob, I felt years bound in wounds and obligations come to the surface. How long did I lay there? How many waves of uncontrolled sobbing came and went? I don't know. I could only lie there paralyzed in emptiness. At some point in the emptiness, I felt the top of my left hand get warm. There was a gentle weight to the warmth on my hand, like someone was holding it. It had been four years since my mother passed. Hearing her voice say *I love you,* and *you're going to be alright* as I lie on my office floor reminded me how much I missed her.

Mom raised my older sister and me to be driven. Like most single parents, she wanted us to have a better life than she could provide. Growing up, struggles were a part of life. Alcoholism and untreated mental health needs were the backbones of our struggles. Early on, I learned to step up and support our family. In our little family unit, I took on the role of the one everyone could rely on, always the dependable one. Even though our situation forced me to grow up quickly, I held tight to a dream of one day working with animals. That dream was mine to capture and live.

A few years after graduating from college, I was hired as a full-time wildlife biologist. As I write this, there are less than 20,000 full-time wildlife biologist jobs in North America. Each year less than two percent of people with degrees in wildlife work as full-time wildlife biologists. That's about the same odds as an athlete playing professional sports. My specific discipline is even rarer. When I was hired, only forty-five of us in North America focused on applied human-wildlife management. In the beginning, I was the only one without an advanced degree in Statistics or at least a decade of field experience and one of only two women in the discipline. I learn to work harder than my colleagues just to keep my job. I thought hard work and extra hours were a fair price to pay to live my dream.

My passion didn't stop with my job. I loved finding the answers to tough problems, and telling the story for wildlife fueled my passion. It consumed my every waking hour. I proudly wore my reputation for getting things done for everyone to see. My reward for working hard and getting things done? More work. Fifty hours a week turned into sixty. Sixty turned into seventy. During the busy times of the year, eighty and ninety-hour workweeks went on for several months in a row. As my workload increased, the more I got wound up in getting work done at the expense of everything else in my life.

Tuesday, September second, was the day my world started to crumble. Just before my ten o'clock conference call, my husband called me. "I'm going to the hospital." He sounded weak. "Why? What's wrong?" "I broke my leg." "Are you sure it's broken?" With his voice getting softer with each word, he said, "Yeah. I don't know what hospital they're taking me." Then the phone went dead. Mike worked construction most of his life and had never had an accident. I didn't know what part of town he was working or who at the job site to call. After frantically driving to five different hospitals throughout the metro area, I finally found him in the ER being prepped for surgery with his left foot attached by only a sliver of skin. After waiting for hours with no updates, the orthopedic surgeon stopped by to let me know that the surgery went well but expected at least 18 months of recovery.

That Friday, my mom called me at work. I had been mostly estranged from her for over fifteen years due to her drinking. "I just saw my doctor. He says I've got a little over a year to live." Shocked, I shouted, "Oh my god, mom! What's going on? What doctor?" Advanced stage four cirrhosis of the liver was the diagnosis. She sounded shocked and confused, "I'm going to need you to help me with things. He says that I forget things like someone with dementia. I need you to help and to check in on me." After our step-father died, my sister thought it was best to move mom near me in case she needed help with anything. We had barely spoken since she moved from out-of-state to two miles away. In just days, I became the primary caregiver of a man who instantly lost his livelihood, and a woman who was rapidly forgetting why I was in her life.

The next year was a blur. I was constantly wound up in trying to be there for everyone. I couldn't keep up with the needs of two households and my job. I threw myself deeper into my work because I was failing at being the caretaker at home.

Mom passed away almost a year from the day she called me with her diagnosis. My life went from crumbling to tailspin. Setbacks and more surgeries for Mike, drawn-out probate for mom's estate, and new demands from work wound me up more and more in my grief. I threw myself deeper into my work. I lived and worked in pure survival mode.

The fall and winter months were a blur. I became more withdrawn with each passing month, focusing only on my work. I was thick into the busiest time of year at work when I realized that I had not cried or grieved my mom's passing—nearly six months since she transitioned, and I had yet to shed a tear. I wanted to cry, bawl, get angry, scream, anything to let out what I had been feeling since her death, but I couldn't. Nothing ever came out. So, I pushed my emotions aside to focus on the whirlwind of work.

By April, my busy time at work had finished, and it was time for annual work performance reviews. My supervisor had retired in December, which created some chaos around who was going to do the performance reviews for many of us. Jim and Doug were already sitting at the small round meeting table as I entered the meeting room for my review. Doug was my interim supervisor, short-timing everything he could until they hired a permanent supervisor. Jim was my supervisor's supervisor. Both were long into the twilight of their careers and were more used to working with male colleagues than female staff.

Doug kicked the meeting off. He chose his words carefully as he walked a tightrope between not saying too much and saying just enough. "You're working too hard. You just need not work so hard. Take a break." Jim interrupted to add how they have plans to support me and that, "You shouldn't work so hard because you could get sick from working too hard."

What a joke. Jim had been with the agency three years in an office just a few doors down from mine. In all of that time, Jim never said hello directly to me or acknowledged that I was part of his staff.

I sat there quietly, stoned-face in awe of Jim and Doug bumbling through my review and any words of wisdom they could think of, no matter the relevance. I don't remember what point in the conversation triggered me, but I was definitely triggered. Wound up so tight from the last couple of years of life I absolutely lost it. *"Are you fucking kidding me?"* I erupted. The spring had been sprung, and there was no going back. "If you had even a remote fucking idea of what I do, you wouldn't even begin to say the shit you just said!" The pain spewed out. Nothing was off-limits. I threw all my personal and professional wounds open raw and exposed them onto the table in an epic level of insubordination. I didn't hold back, and neither did the meeting room walls. They let my volcanic rage pass right through them for everyone in the office to hear.

"We'll get you some help. I can have Ginny help with any mailings you need done," was Jim's feeble attempt at de-escalation. Not to be outdone by Jim, Doug volleyed with his own attempt to deescalate, "I'll have Jody help with whatever she can help with." I could feel my head ready to explode. Every muscle in my body was tense as I pushed my face within inches of Jim's face. Through clenched jaws, I countered their attempts. "Everything I do is electronic. I do not have *any* fucking mailings! You barely know my name, and you for damn sure don't know my job!" My rage brought me within a whisper of physically striking Jim. My clenched fist slammed the top of the table as I stormed out of the meeting. Every wall in that part of the building shook as my office door slammed shut. Fuming, I plopped into my piece of shit chair, tears rolling down my face.

Less than a minute later, I got a text from a colleague down the hall, "Why don't you go home and take a few days off?"

That day I was lucky I didn't get fired. I was lucky I didn't get charged with assault. I was lucky I didn't get written up by Human Resources. A higher power must have been looking out for me because that day, I was beyond lucky!

That day was also when I realized my career, the dream job so many want, was no longer my dream. I was done.

The next several weeks were spent on my couch, shedding tears that would not stop, screaming the pain of unrecoverable loss, pleading for another chance to change the past, and questioning everything that had been my life up until that point. I was grieving the loss of my mom, and I was grieving the loss of my dream. Grief brought me into emptiness with no boundaries, definition, purpose, or motivation. The only sensation that existed came from the wounds I was now aware of raw and weeping from their time wound up in darkness.

Weeks into the emptiness, I started to hear *write it out* over and over in my head. After several days of hearing this repeated phrase, I found a pen and notepad from my mom's house on the bookshelf by the couch. As I picked them up, my hand instantly started writing "We love you," and "Everything is perfect, you are perfect," over and over, covering every inch of the page. Page after page, the identical phrases came out. The words fell onto the page effortlessly, but I was not the one telling my hand to write. I could see my hand holding the pen writing, but I did not feel my arm or hand.

Over the next four days, I sat on the couch, pen and paper in hand, as the same phrases repeatedly fell onto the pages. As I read those words covering the papers strewn around me, I felt a light and direction within the emptiness for the first time. Hour after hour, I held the pen to any piece of paper I could find. Hour after hour, "We love you," and "Everything is perfect, you are perfect," were effortlessly scribed. As the hours and days went by, my grief transformed into the possibility of escaping from the emptiness. I started to breathe again without the burden of life winding around me. I felt hope for the first time in years.

The couch had transformed from a wallow of emptiness into my place of hope and possibilities. Day after day, my life centered around the messages magically scribed on paper. One morning like every morning before, I jumped out of bed and raced to the couch to witness the messages. This time nothing happened. *Was I holding the pen wrong? No. Maybe I needed a different piece of paper? Nope, not that either.* I was deflated, staring at the empty paper in my lap.

As the emptiness drifted back over me, I felt someone looking at me. I knew I was alone in the house, but I couldn't shake the feeling of being stared at. I took a deep breath and looked up from the paper. My mom was standing there before me, young and healthy, as real as you and me. In a strong, gentle voice, she said, "Hello, my darling, are you ready to get to work?" I instinctively said yes as I rose from the couch with arms stretched out to give her a hug. She disappeared before I could reach her. That day I knew hope and possibilities would always be part of my life.

"Mary, are you alright?" It was Erik outside my office door. "I know you didn't make the decision to retire lightly. You're the glue to our team, and we love you for that." He paused. "Don't worry. Everything will be perfect in its own way. You're going to be okay."

In the months since telling Erik of my retirement, I've learned the more we let go of what winds us up and bounds us in wounds, the more we heal and the closer we get to the effortless magic that surrounds us every day.

Now when someone asks what I'm going to do in retirement, I look at them with a soft smile, and confidently say, "Oh, I'm not retiring. I'm rewiring. I've spent too many years being something I thought I needed to be. I was living the dream, so many others want to live. I got so wound up doing everything to get the most done. I wound up trying to be there for everyone else so much, that I lost myself. So, I'm going to rewire, share the magic that surrounds us, and I'm going to unwind."

Mary Lloyd is a medium and animal intuitive. As a natural medium and channeler, Mary blends practical and spiritual messages to assist others in finding and putting the pieces of their life's puzzle together. She's a certified Reiki teacher and animal communicator. With a degree in Ethology, the study of animal behavior, Mary spent nearly 30 years as a career biologist in wildlife and natural resource management. Her time as a wildlife professional gave her unique insight into how humans affect wildlife and wildlife affect humans.

She was spiritually asleep until her mother's death reawakened her awareness and gifts of connecting with other dimensions and possibilities. Mary dedicates her time to bringing voices of animals and nature into everyday life and introducing others to the effortless magic that surrounds us every day.

Contact Mary on:

Website: marylloydmedium.com

FB: Mary Lloyd Medium

Instagram: @MaryLloydMedium

CHAPTER 11

I AM AN ALCHEMIST

DISMANTLING MY FAMILY'S PROGRAMS AND DISCOVERING I AM MY OWN MEDICINE

Thais Krause, Holistic Wellness Coach and Reiki Master

"You are a monster. I won't accept this inside of my house! Get out of here! Go live with your father! You're just like him, his sister, and his mother! You just can't seem to learn how to be any better than that! Don't be so loud. You're so rude!"

Those were my mother's words, shouted in anger with a grimace on her face that prevented her mouth from containing the lasting cigarette smoke within her lungs.

It all started after my parents' divorce when I was seven years old. The emotional outbursts and physical punishments went on for years. I grew up asking for forgiveness for being who I was. Throughout what seemed like a never-ending saga of my parents' divorce chaos, I grew to believe it was my responsibility to make my mother happy. She would often strangle my arms tightly and utter claims such as "I do everything for you!" She would question me. "Why do you treat me this way?" "What way?" I might say in response.

The reasoning, I suppose, was that I loved my father, and I had a strong resemblance to him, whether I could acknowledge it or not. To her, my father was a useless, irresponsible man, and I was guilty of betrayal. "You glorify him! You are out of your mind!" She'd say.

Yet, I loved my father dearly, as I loved her. He, in contrast, was naturally cheery and outgoing, which made hating him impossible for me. I was torn. Countless were the days that I wandered through my elementary school's hallways, wondering in variable angst why I was the only child often seen puffy-eyed and red-faced, with barely a voice. I questioned whether anyone else was going through the same turmoil. It didn't seem so, which added layers of disappointment and want.

My childhood years went on like this for a decade. Their fighting never ceased, and money was tight. My father didn't help financially. My mother was a fountain of never-ending blame and regret. While I had many happy moments with the members of both sides of my family, they all engaged in emotional fights, and the drama prevailed. Their dealings dragged me down. But I grew used to it. I carried a deep sense of sadness within me. However, I was strong, and by the grace of God, I never lamented in my woes for very long. Instead, I turned towards my extra-familiar activities with a zeal that brought me much joy, many friendships, sports, and an appreciation for a time in nature.

I discovered that the Catholic church in my father's neighborhood brought me solace and comfort. At mass, my heart would swell with hope as the tears ran down when we sang lovely hymns. I would feel connected to Jesus through an appreciation for his suffering. I mumbled the lyrics, half sobbing. I joined the youth group. *Please, God, bring peace to my family.* Yet, my prayers were remained unanswered, at least for a moment.

To make matters worse, my mother's father died quickly of harsh cancer. We witnessed him transform from the strong householder we knew, to rotting in a hospital bed. My mother was heartbroken once again.

During a summer break, I had spent a week with my father, and when I came back home, I found my mother asleep in the same pajamas she was in when I left. Cigarettes filled an ashtray to the brim, and a two-liter Coca-Cola bottle sat empty next to her bed. It looked as though she had only gotten up to pee during the entire week, I was absent. It was around this time that my mother turned to pharmaceuticals and things shifted from bad to worse.

At 14 years old, I knew what it meant to have a mother who was severely depressed. An entire year passed, and not much changed until mother received a new job opportunity in Rio de Janeiro. I was dumbstruck! We left our small hometown to try something new. *Wow, what an amazing place to be!* I thought to myself when we arrived in the city.

My heart swelled with joy as I jogged on the beach boardwalk. I felt so alive! There was live music everywhere, people playing volleyball on the hot sand, and laughter was heard everywhere. We could see the ocean from our bedroom window, and life in the big city was better than it had ever been, at least for me.

Shortly after moving, God sent me a spark that lit a flame in my heart. It came in the form of a young man who would turn out to be all that I needed to begin my journey of healing. The spark came on one summer night while my mother and I were out for a walk by the beach. A group of four Americans happened to be beside us, having a snack when serendipitously we all found ourselves in conversation.

Little did I know I had met my soul mate and the father of my children. Billy and I fell deeply in love. He made me feel like it was ok to be me. "I like to be with you, my beautiful little Brazilian babe!" He whispered while looking intensely into my eyes. When we met, I was only 15 years old, but our love felt more mature than that. His presence in my life allowed me to start discovering the essence of who I was. I could forget my family's drama. I even started to realize the problems were theirs, not mine.

After four years of spending our summers together, we got married. I was off to America, never having traveled outside of the country. My destiny awaited me. Love, and a brave new world far from my family's never-ending turmoil, that until that time, had never ceased to be the bane of my existence.

I lived the American dream. Life was good as a wife and college student. Sadly, my mother's life changed for the worse. After an episode of physical abuse, she ended her relationship with her boyfriend. She became empty-nested and heartbroken.

Despite the distance, my mother continued to impose her problems on me incessantly. She was lonely, her emphysema started showing itself, and she was constantly in physical discomfort. I began to share all I was learning in college about the physical body and ways to bring health back to it. She barely acknowledged it and returned to complain about her life.

In my mother's mind, life was not worth living. She tried to end her life twice but wasn't courageous enough to add alcohol to her poisonous recipe of hundreds of Xanax. A few years later, her brother died of cancer, and she became a breast cancer survivor. The cancers in my family raised so many questions for me. *Why is it happening to my family more than everyone else I know?* I wondered.

I immersed myself in research and learned about toxicity. I shared with my mother about all the possible external causes of cancer. "I will do better," she moaned as she puffed another cigarette, drank another glass of coke, and continued with her sedentary, pill-popping lifestyle. I grew in immense frustration because she took zero steps to get better yet continued to complain daily. I blamed her for the physical condition she was in. The dichotomy was clear, and the distance between us grew greater. While I was beginning to find the light through my discovery of holistic health, the bane of my existence had not subsided.

A friend suggested hosting a full moon gathering for women in my house in January of 2020. For the first time, I had the realization that other women had gone through great struggles and were also working on their healing. I exploded into tears when it was my time to share. I wanted to let go of the guilt and the shame for not being good enough for my mother and of my lifetime frustration trying to fix her with no success.

Among these women, I felt heard and held. Tiffany's voice and mannerisms most resonated with me. I wanted to feel as peaceful as she looked. That day taught me that I needed to let go of the pain I was carrying if I wanted to be the most loving mother I desired. The shadows of my past came to the surface when I lost patience with my two small children. I realized I carried anger inside. I unconsciously showed my anxious behavior towards the little people I most loved. On the outside, I looked happy, but deep inside, a heaviness resided in my heart.

In 2021, I had an opportunity to participate in a healing program, and I spontaneously enrolled. *How to Heal* was channeled from the light spirits. This course brought the answers to all my childhood prayers and the healing I was looking for. The understanding that past lives traumas affect this current lifetime brought solace to my heart.

I remember my mother often mentioned that she had never had a joyful heart since she was a little girl. I began to comprehend that her suffering may have resulted from a past life. *It is her soul that needs healing, not her physical body or mind.* I thought. Through forgiveness and love, I began my healing journey. I prayed for forgiveness and forgave any souls I may have hurt in all my lifetimes, including the current one. The heaviness in my heart started to dissolve. I began to feel compassion for my mother. She, too, was a sister in darkness, needing more love, light, compassion, and forgiveness to her soul.

I practiced speaking with love, listening, acknowledging, being present, accepting myself and others for the divinity that we are. It was everything I wanted to experience as a child. I gave it all to myself and others. I began to bring attention to the words I spoke, loudly and silently in my head. For every complaint, I asked myself, *How can I bring gratitude to this experience? Can I look at it from a different perspective?*

I was in awe of how much I had learned! Every suffering became a lesson. I realized that I am much more powerful than the church taught me. Knowing that I cannot be my highest self if I allow guilt, shame, anxiety, and victimhood to take place inside of me was liberating. I spent years taking care of my physical body with fear of cancer, only to discover that cancer, like all diseases, begins with our emotions, the energies in motion. I began doing more to raise my vibration. I started to feel lighter and lighter. My mother still lived an unfulfilled life without leaving her apartment, but I didn't feel ashamed of experiencing immense joy.

My ego started to calm down. I felt less need to prove I was right and tell my mother what to do. There is no right or wrong. There are only experiences and the beliefs we take from those experiences. I told her about my need to experience life differently and how I made a conscious decision to shift my behavior in a two-hour phone conversation filled with compassion, gentle teachings, and emotional release. We asked each other for forgiveness. An immense weight came off my shoulders. Now I was free to share my happiness with her.

With my newfound lightness, I turned towards connecting with Spirit. Nature became more magical. As I ran on the trail among the tall skinny trees, a woodpecker flew right in front of me. It was a message of spiritual healing, perseverance, and strength. The woodpecker sees hope even in a dead tree. For years, I felt my mother was dead, or at least not living. I knew I was being guided by the Light.

On a summer day, I took my daughter out for a special girl's date. My friend placed the massage table out in the yard. The cicadas were out by the hundreds, the sun was shining through the tall trees, and the wind blew the branches. My 5-year-old daughter chose to receive Reiki first. She laid there for 15 minutes, motionless, eyes closed.

After her session, something shifted. My previously over-anxious little girl sat calmly, listening at long last, to our conversation about auras and chakras. That night she said to me before bed, "Mommy, I really like Reiki. You know when you go to church, eat that little bread, and connect with God in your heart? I feel like I met God today." My eyes watered. How beautiful that she could feel God's love through that session! It had made an impact on her behavior. The next day I woke up certain that Reiki could be an ally in emotional healing.

The day came for me to have a private session with the medium that taught "How to Heal." The room was bright, filled with plants and crystals. Spirit spoke through her. *"Why are you here?"* I sighed as the tears started to roll down. "All I have wanted was for my mom to get better and stop suffering. My biggest frustration is I could not help her. Her health is so poor. She suffered two recent heart attacks. She can't work. How can it be that people pay me to be their trainer and help them detox, yet despite my best efforts, my mother is the sickest person I know?" I was sobbing. "I have this deep longing to heal people." The medium smiled. "You have lived many lives. In every life, you were a healer, a plant medicine woman. In this life, you will be working with your hands." My jaw dropped. I had not told anyone but my husband I started studying Reiki.

Deep inside, I had always yearned to be a healer. I always felt like one but only acted in the physical body through movement and food. I had struggled with my expression. I had to dig much deeper to truly help people become their happiest, healthiest, most fulfilled selves. I had to support their souls and their energy bodies.

This experience solidified my resolve and drove me deeper into holistic coaching and mastering Reiki. We are a soul, an energy body, a mind, and a physical body entangled in a dance that can be a dream or nightmare. My heartfelt calm, my anxiety was gone, I quit drinking alcohol. I sat in silence with my sage while feeling the presence of the angels around me. I was living a dream.

This awakening to my soul's purpose happened during the global pandemic. The state of the world drove me to intensify my resolution. My husband and I realized our lives in Maryland were more materialistic and matrix-driven than our hearts desired. We were ready to move our family to the water. To my surprise, my dad and his spouse of twenty years left their stable lives in my hometown to move to Florida too.

While immersed in my healing, having my father and his wife living with us was overwhelming. I felt I had healed, but my father's presence triggered a lot within me. His ego spoke louder than my now calm heart. I was astounded to realize that some of what I was deprogramming from came from him, not my mother. As a child, I had only spent every other weekend with him, doing fun things. Living together as adults brought a whole new perspective.

One day, I had an emotional outburst and acted just like my 30-something-year-old mother used to. At that moment, I knew why Spirit sent my dad here at this exact time in my life. I could feel the injustice and anger my mother felt. I couldn't contain it inside my chest. I felt so unappreciated by him and his wife after welcoming them with open arms into my home. I screamed, "If your wife can't forgive me over an argument, then you must leave my house." My heart raced, and I saw the story repeating itself. This time, I was the one yelling and kicking somebody out. I cried loudly as I hated every minute of it while also acknowledging that I was projecting years of pain and victimhood onto them.

In Florida, I encountered so many opportunities for healing in the community. Spirit guided me to a full moon gathering, where I met a soul sister. After a couple of ceremonies together and coffee dates, she asked me, "What about your Reiki practice? Can you give me Reiki?" Shivers went down my spine. I almost didn't have the courage to answer.

The fight with my father had numbed me. I felt unworthy of bringing forth healing as I realized I still carried so much inside. *Why did I allow their behavior to upset me?* I wondered if I was on the right path. I questioned the Reiki symbols. I pressed on the breaks. "Who am I to channel healing energy? I am not pure." My friend proceeded to say, "Thais, you are love. Your intention is what matters the most. Healing is your dharma. I would love for you to give me Reiki." I'm sure Spirit was speaking through her. I accepted. I dove deeper into my Reiki studies. After my session with her, I felt ready to continue my healing and give the gift of Reiki to my friends. After many ancestor prayers, sitting with my inner child, daily Reiki sessions, and profoundly forgiving, I started to see I was positively impacting myself and others.

Women started requesting my coaching to assist in their healing. Our sessions, guided by the light, helped women gain clarity and perspective about their suffering. It was beautiful to witness. I launched my holistic coaching business. Embodying the healer that my soul so desired made my days magical.

In January of 2022, exactly two years after my first full moon circle, I led a full moon gathering on the beach alongside my soul sister. I channeled Reiki to the attendees while the crystal sound bowls vibrated the frequency of love. The moon was bright in the sky, its light reflecting on the ocean waves. The veil between the Earth and spiritual world had been lifted, and I could so feel it that night. It was chilly on the beach. Even though I was wearing a puffy sweater and yoga pants, my soul felt as if I were in an ancient ceremony, flowing in a long dress. I felt so at home, as if I had done that before. I surrendered to Spirit as it was clear that my path in life was going towards healing others. *I am open to receiving. Show me. Guide me.*

As of now, it feels I have deprogrammed from my family's story and recreated my own. My mother became open to my suggestions more than ever. I talk her through meditative healing journeys and give her weekly distant Reiki sessions. My goal is no longer to fix her but to love her soul. Our relationship is repaired. We can laugh on the phone again, and my six-year-old daughter's behavior has also improved. Perhaps it is a combination of bedtime Reiki sessions and having a more compassionate mother.

The night before I finished writing this chapter, my daughter said to me before bed, "Momma, parents teach kids, then kids become parents and teach their kids, then they have kids and teach their kids? That's how you learn to be a parent?" My heart swelled, and I took a deep breath. "Yes, except if you don't like the way your parents taught you, you can teach a new way to your kids." She smiled and replied with a long hug, "I'm going to teach my kids just like my mama teaches me." I broke out into tears. At that moment, I knew I had broken the cycle. She always tells me I am the best mama ever. In surrendering to Spirit, I was able to alchemize my life. Now I know for certain the only way to heal is to be my own medicine.

Thais has spent the last 12 years dedicating her career to the physical body. She became a certified personal trainer in 2010 and received a degree in Kinesiology from the University of Maryland in 2013. She has completed multiple continuing education courses, workshops, and seminars for improving physical health. She holds certificates in various fitness categories such as mobility training, strength training, postural alignment, pain management, nutrition for improved physical performance, and gut health for immune system support.

In 2020, after experiencing her own spiritual awakening and inner healing, Thais expanded her field to include holistic health and energy healing practices. She became a certified holistic wellness coach and Reiki Master. She's passionate about how nutrition, movement, energy healing, and spirituality work beautifully to heal the mind, body, and soul.

Today Thais is a lifestyle transformation coach! She gives her clients the tools they need to deprogram from their limitations to create the highest version of themselves. Stay connected with Thais, through:

Instagram: @nature.intended.wellness

Website: natureintendedwellness.com

CHAPTER 12

YOU WERE MADE FOR THIS

HOW I EVOLVED MY INNER TEACHER WITH CONFIDENCE AND HUMILITY

Sheri Welsh, MPS, RYT-200, RCYT-95

It was a warm and sticky August afternoon in Columbia, Maryland. The air conditioning cooled my skin inside the brick corporate office building. The fluorescent lights made everything in the conference room look artificial and bleak. I rolled out most of the armchairs into the hallway, moved the tables to the perimeter of the room, and set up my mat, speaker, and singing bowl. This was my way of creating some warmth and enough space for the ten students who had signed up for their very first yoga class at my place of work, a health care company. The very first yoga class the company offered in its 25+ year history. And the very first yoga class I would teach since becoming a certified instructor two years prior.

I glanced over at the standard wall clock above the entrance. I could feel the secondhand tick in my core and echo in my skull as it inched towards the 5:15 p.m. mark. *This is it; no turning back now. Shit—am I really cut out for this?* I took a deep breath in and let it out with a smile and warm welcome as I scanned the room of familiar and not-so-familiar faces—nothing artificial and bleak about the bodies that sat before me, eagerly awaiting my instruction and guidance.

Despite having earned a graduate degree in public relations, I never fully overcame my fear of public speaking. Somehow that day, the light radiating from the students before me brought me genuine comfort and a hint of confidence. The class was a hit, and I walked away feeling exhilarated and enthusiastic for next week.

From that point on and through to today, I often seek teaching inspiration from the outside, like social media and other teachers. Two years before my first teaching gig, I attended a regular Iyengar Yoga class in Bethesda, Maryland. Iyengar focuses on stringent alignment, teacher demonstration, and heavy use of props to attain the utmost expression of the asana (pose) in an individual body. While the Iyengar tradition influenced my teaching in the short term, I knew I wanted to grow and incorporate other styles and somehow seek inspiration from *within*.

Eventually, I branched out and became a student of other styles— Vinyasa, Hatha, Restorative, Prenatal, Yin, and Hot Yoga. I picked and chose what worked best for me as I explored my personal teaching style. After one year leading corporate yoga, the class size had dwindled down to two regular students, and we decided to suspend the program. At first, I felt disheartened but reminded myself all things are cyclical, with a beginning and an end. I was deeply grateful to have the opportunity to connect with the beautiful souls who committed to practicing with me every Wednesday afternoon for an entire year. I was grateful to myself for committing to teach them.

I continued my personal practice and even took one-off special event gigs from time to time. One fateful day in sunny Bethesda, I stepped into a hot yoga studio, and my teacher journey changed forever.

I set up my mat at the 95-degree studio and took a class with Micah, the owner. He was tall, lithe, and had comforting eyes. I immediately noticed the black and red tattoo sleeves draping his right arm and leg: Sanskrit-style lettering decorated the word "Vinyasa" on his forearm and an intricate mandala canopied his knee cap.

Over the next 60 minutes, sweat accumulated on my mat, and I immediately regretted not bringing my towel. I engaged neglected muscles as a means to prevent myself from slipping and smashing my face on the slick thermoplastic. My face contorted with every challenging move and relaxed with each long exhale. Still, I was in awe of Micah's grace, expertise, bold diction, and clear direction. I came back for more and explored other teachers and their unique styles. The humility I experienced during each heated class was overwhelming, so I created space to absorb and evolve in my mind and body.

One day, I walked in to find the words "Teacher Tryouts" written in large stylish letters on the floor-to-ceiling chalkboard by the sunlit studio front entrance. It was like a message from the heavens. *Do it,* my inner voice (and Micah) encouraged; meanwhile, my brain talked me out of it. My mind concocted a standard—an expectation that didn't exist—to which I had to seemingly meet. The other teachers seemed so confident and capable. *Can I teach in a heated studio?*

How many times has an opportunity fallen into *your* lap as you witness your insecurities talk you out of it? How many times have you let your fear talk you out of confidently striding forward? I meditated on the possibility of teaching at the studio for many nights.

I emailed Micah, "I'm going to do it!". Taking this leap of faith *in writing* would make it more definitive and less likely I'd back out and continue with my safe, cozy life. When the day came, I stepped into a room full of teachers and members of the community. I auditioned with five others, whose individual styles shined as brightly as themselves. I felt unusually calm. "I'll go first," I said, raising my hand. All eyes were on me, eagerly awaiting my instruction and guidance. *This feels familiar,* thinking back to that first class in Columbia.

While teaching my sequence, I heard a whisper coming from the back row. An older woman politely mouthed "speak up!" while gesturing her thumb upward. The acoustics in the studio seemed to amplify my voice already. She gestured again. Then again. I smiled back politely and my chest tightened as I felt my calming voice escalate to an almost-yell. I glanced over at Micah and he nodded with approval each time I consciously spoke louder, which brought me comfort and unwound the tightness in my chest. *This is way harder than I remember,* I thought to myself. I had my work cut out for me.

I wrote Micah a thank you email the next day, which was followed by a couple of days of agonizing radio silence. Just when I was about to give up hope, my inbox pinged me with a new message from Micah.

"Hi Sheri! I'd like to offer you a spot in our 60-day mentorship program, *Refine,* where I'd like you to pair you up with me! The intention is to support you as a teacher, get you ready to teach a class here at the studio and team up with us!

I was overjoyed. *Does this experienced yogi want to be **my** mentor?* A rush of confidence blanketed me. We met weekly in a small office at the back of the studio, furnished only with a small shelf of props, a couple of rolling chairs and a whiteboard scribbled with ideas. Micah handed me a "Journey to Power" script to study and better understand the Baptiste style of teaching. He one-on-one critiqued my teaching, answered every single one of my questions, and asked me to provide hands-on adjustments to students during a couple of his jam-packed classes.

When it was my time to shine, I taught a Friday morning community class averaging five students several weeks in a row. Some familiar faces, some new. With each passing week, my pre-class butterflies seemed to settle and my post-class buzz left me soaring higher. The day after my fifth and final community class, the world abruptly shut down due to the COVID-19 pandemic. I couldn't help but think, *this opportunity couldn't have come at a more perfect time.*

Equipped with my new sense of confidence and direction, I launched my yoga business and applied all I learned from my mentorship. I offered various nonprofits free online yoga to increase their brand awareness—a skill I had learned in my 15-year career as a marketer and communicator. The word yoga means to yoke or join, mind, body, and soul. While I happily connect my students with a true sense of peace and inner fierce, I also strive to strike a healthy balance of confidence and humility within myself.

My voice of doubt revisited me upon relocating to Lake Tahoe the following year. Here in this destination town, sprinkled year-round with tourists from all walks of life: *Could I live up to the title of Yoga Teacher?* I stepped away from a lucrative marketing career to focus on motherhood and teaching yoga, so, naturally, the answer to my own question had to be a resounding yes!

This dance of hesitancy and self-encouragement reminded me of my first time attending a women's circle in Washington DC several years ago. A dear friend and lightworker invited me to join a small gathering of women led by a shaman to manifest our deepest dreams and desires. I came equipped with a journal, pen, and open mind. The group was warm and welcoming and threw around phrases like "as above, so below," "cords," and "ascension," most of which I had never heard. I immediately doubted myself. *Do I really belong here?*

The circle quite literally revolved around guided meditation practice, something I *did* have some experience with, so I decided to stick with it. We took turns meditating for one another. When someone was chosen, they and the rest of the group would partake in a guided meditation and then journal and share what they experienced or saw immediately after.

Cora, the young and fair-skinned brunette to my right, was the subject of one of my meditations, and I remember seeing a beautiful greenhouse in my mind's eye. In this scene, an older lady appeared with light emanating all around her and gorgeous blossoms surrounding her in every corner. A bluebird appeared and perched on her shoulder, portraying a sense of deep calm both in her and in myself.

When it was time for me to share with Cora what I saw, she let out a waterfall of tears. "That was my mother who visited you. She passed away last year," she confided. "She absolutely *loved* bluebirds."

I was shocked. Was it pure coincidence that these images happened to correlate with Cora's recent experiences? "You have a gift," Cora later whispered to me. "I hope you take time to explore it." There I was, feeling like a total newbie, yet the answers already existed within me. I just needed to step into my confidence.

As the years passed, I gradually realized *we all* have vast wells of untapped potential within us. It's a matter of keeping an open mind and stepping out of our comfort zones to recognize and realize that true potential.

Once we were settled into our Lake Tahoe home, opportunities arose, and I found myself teaching at two studios, a daycare, and a world-renowned resort. The physical, mental, and emotional toll of teaching more than three to four classes a week was deeply humbling at first. I would come home at the end of the week and doze off on the couch while my three-year-old daughter quietly played with her toys. My presence at home was slipping through my fingers as I became all-encompassed with the world of teaching yoga. I swiftly set boundaries on a maximum number of weekly classes so I could continue to care for my daughter and stay present for myself and my family.

Occasionally, my confidence must be handheld out of the shadows and back into my consciousness. At one of the studios where I teach, we must live stream our classes. Each time I record a class, I watch after and critique myself with the intention of learning from my mistakes and becoming a better teacher. Once in a while, harsh internal dialogue seeps through:

Geez, why'd you pick that pants and top combo? Your fat is poking out!

Your voice is too soft. Speak up!

That hairstyle makes your forehead look big.

You're mumbling far too much for anyone to understand you.

My therapist recommended an exercise where I audio record myself critiquing my teaching videos in real-time. To my surprise, *it worked.* Releasing negative self-talk can sometimes help identify the root of where it comes from. By meeting our harsh inner critic and emitting negative thoughts into the universe or on paper, we are uprooting the weight which holds us back from reaching our true, blooming potential. We can also turn self-criticism into constructive feedback. In watching myself teach, I learned to make a concerted effort to speak more clearly and focus on the *practice,* not the vessel.

Whenever I notice the negativity creep in now, I deliberately exercise more positive self-talk:

Check out that funky and creative transition!

You give students permission to explore for themselves through a healthy balance of instruction and silence.

That color looks fantastic on you and really allows your radiance to shine through.

Your alignment is impeccable!

Can we quiet our harsh inner critic *just enough* to learn from our experiences without dimming our light? Can we amplify our positive self-talk *just enough* to fuel our passions without becoming arrogant? This ebb and flow, much like vinyasa's connection of breath with movement, can be a powerful tool to help us expand our heart, our intuition, and our inner fierce.

The ebb and flow of confidence and humility is the balance that keeps my teaching fresh, motivated, and inspired. My inner teacher is more than just a yoga practitioner. She is a clear communicator and a spiritual cheerleader. She is a focused, present listener and works every day to incorporate this quality into all corners of her life. She also takes time to sit in silence and observe her mind.

She is inquisitive, analytical, and a problem solver. When moments of humility surface, she expands her borders and welcomes with an open heart opportunities to learn, achieve, and manifest more. When her confidence soars, her inner voice proudly states:

You were made for this!

Sheri was born in Tehran, Iran, just a couple of years after the revolution. Her parents left the country and raised their two children in the outskirts of New York, Philadelphia, and Washington, DC. She started practicing yoga in 2007 to seek balance in her runner's body and anxious mind. She became a certified yoga teacher at Pilgrimage of the Heart yoga studio in San Diego six years later. After becoming a mother in 2017, she wanted to find ways to better connect with her daughter. Sheri left her 15+ year marketing career to focus on motherhood and her overall well-being and became a registered children's yoga teacher in 2019.

Sheri studied classical piano for almost ten years at the prestigious Levine School of Music in Washington, DC. After high school, she graduated with a bachelor's degree in English from the University of Maryland, Baltimore County (UMBC). After a five-year career as a technical writer, she enrolled in Georgetown University's School of Continuing Studies' Public Relations and Corporate Communications program to receive her Master of Professional Studies (MPS). She studied part-time while working full-time and even traveled a semester abroad to work closely with a global marketing firm in London.

In 2020, Sheri and her little family of three left their lives in Washington, DC and traveled across the country in an RV, settling in beautiful Zephyr Cove, Nevada, a mile up the road from Lake Tahoe. She teaches students of all ages and abilities at various studios and daycares. You can find her outside daily for a walk, run, mountain bike, hike, snowshoe, snowboard, swim, or riding her SUP on the lake.

Learn more about Sheri's offerings at www.fierceheronyoga.com and follow her travel blog at www.welshsvoyagewest.com.

CHAPTER 13

FULLY EMBODIED / FIERCELY EMPOWERED

SPIRITUAL GROWTH THROUGH ILLNESS AND PAIN

Kelbi McCumber Morris,
Quantum Energy Facilitator, Shamanic Healer

At this point, I've been horizontal for most of a decade. I've remained held in this dark embrace, sinking, disassociating, unfeeling myself in all the ways—lost and accustomed to misery.

I was feeding off of the cycle of mind traps, knowing it could go on forever if I let it. I was alone in my bed with my thoughts wrapped up in the fetal position in my own cocoon of sheets, sweat, and fear. It's getting hot—suffocating hot. But I didn't come out. I don't dare break the seal of this uncomfortable comfort zone. No way. I know this place. I know what to expect here, even if it's not what I want. So, I don't reach for a breath or stick a toe out to feel any cool salvation. I just stay—languishing. Safe? Questionable. Same? Absolutely. I have known this, even if it's not desirable. The fear of any more unknowns is too great to face—even change. I desperately need change.

I succumbed to my health journey and was buried underneath diagnosis after diagnosis. I took on a new identity with some of those labels, letting some diseases define me and steal my sovereignty. I stuffed myself down, afraid to be me, to be even more misunderstood and outcast.

Because I was not following my north node, my highest path, I became sick. It started with small things bubbling up within me: GERD, foot pains, brain fog, body aches, tiny entry points to much bigger suffering. Having never been encouraged to express my true self, my essence, I was more than repressed, and I completely disassociated from myself, life, and especially my body. I gathered long lists of symptoms and diagnoses, paired with lists of doctors, specialists, treatments, and therapies. I walked with a cane. I had so many medications to consume throughout the day, injections to administer, side effects on top of symptoms, and no hope. They don't give that out at the doctor's office alongside words, letters, and abbreviations like: autoimmune, RA, stage 3 Lyme, endometriosis, cancer, DDD, incurable, and lifelong.

My body was a war zone, not a fun or comfortable place to be. They believed I was doomed to this life and wanted me to believe the same. Ah, an epiphany, a choice: my belief systems need to change!

I am deeply loved, had a great childhood, and well, a life of inhibition.

I did not hold myself in high regard. I did not listen to myself and was not heard by others. I was shy, and for years I denied my truth and the emotions of being misunderstood. There were years of not knowing my needs and having no way to meet them. That's how I got there—under the covers, sick and tired of being sick and tired, miserable in the same horizontal cycle of my life in which one trip to the mailbox with my cane was a great accomplishment—seriously. This was my 30s, not what I'd call my prime by any stretch.

As I lay there, the suffocation starting to take hold, my care about it waning, I heard a cry. At first, I held my breath to listen, thinking it might be my infant crying out for her mother to hold her, feed her, or mother her. But it wasn't. The voice was much closer and yet much farther away. As I began to breathe again, I heard it more clearly. She was meek and muffled, with an undercurrent of determination, strength to be heard. Huh? *Who is this foreign frequency crying out softly?* This was me, my inner child. My cave of bedsheet covers filled with orange light as if I had a flashlight under here with me. I felt it emanating from me, my belly and sacral center. As I allowed this light to cover and consume me, I heard my inner voice again, slightly clearer.

Enough. Time to shine your light. For she will thrive best when I am the lighthouse to guide her, and I will thrive only when my light shines its brightest.

I woke up, unearthed from my den of despair and taking in deep, cool breaths of air. Feeling my skin on the sheets, actually feeling my body on the bed, for the first time in years. My eyes opened to new realizations, beliefs, and desires. When my baby did cry out for me, I answered her call and showed up for us both—realizing that the key to this escape room was within me.

This dark night of the soul was my first awakening.

That day, I decided I wanted embodiment and to feel empowered. This wasn't just a switch to flip, and presto, I'd be back in action. Much like a doctor's treatment plan, spiritual healing takes time. This would take time and effort, and I had to believe in my worth to make this shift happen. I had to adjust my belief system to know I could live again and that I was capable. Easier said than done.

My first leap into spiritual self-discovery came early in those years of suffering when I was introduced to Reiki. This practice put me in control. Feeling the power of the reins in my own hands. Learning a technique I could use on my own was not just appealing but empowering! During this year of learning and discovering energy in a whole new way, as a religion, I also discovered my body possesses its own innate healing ability. This was a fresh concept in my world and woke me wide open! I honestly thought that only doctors healed illness. In case you still have that in your belief system, I'm here to tell you they don't! They *can* be excellent guides and helpers in loads of cases.

I began to meditate often on this new concept with basic guided meditations, quiet music, and breathwork, and witnessed my belief systems around my body and health begin to change. I started to believe in this innate healing for my body and emotions. I began to flourish, knowing I was not trapped in my body. My body is a vessel to be honored, gently cared for, and respected in the highest regard. I didn't know that before. Slowly, I began to see that I had worth—loads of it, worth revealed by every aspect of my essence. Along this journey, I had begun to see myself as trustworthy.

Learning Reiki back in 1999, I had zero peers who knew what the hell I was into or why. I had no one to coregulate with or from whom to find understanding or reassurance. *Am I okay? Am I doing the right thing? Is this even real? Are they judging me? Why can't they just go along for the ride like I have to? I feel so alone.* Doubt continued.

The same could be said for most of my belief systems: my belief in magic, energy, and things unseen. Since childhood, I cannot remember anyone ever engaging me or encouraging me in my daydreams or my unordinary beliefs. This caused me to suppress my magic and disassociate from my body and mind.

This lack of relationship is just one of many examples in my life where I wasn't seen and therefore left myself. In shamanism, we call these moments of life soul loss. In modern psychology, we call it disassociation. I wasn't here anymore; Kelbi had left the body repeatedly, unknowingly.

A mentor once told me, "You spend a lot of time in the other realms, but I get the impression that you don't even know you're there."

I often escaped with my intuitive abilities as part of my disassociation, part of my evasion from human reality and suffering, and part of my healing. I wasn't mad about that, but I did want to participate fully now that I knew I was not only capable but already journeying before I'd ever met my first drum.

I was burnt out on having to prove myself. The patriarchy demands that we earn our worth through strenuous work. I had made my way into the commercial photo industry, a very cutthroat, shallow, image-driven industry—very patriarchal, and not very Kelbi. This is what I went to school for. I knew how to do my job. I was good at it. I felt I should follow this path I paid to be educated in, no matter how uncomfortable it was or how frustrated and burnt out I became.

Gotta save face, I should do what I told my family, peers, the world, I set out to do.

Should's galore! Even if it didn't serve me. Even if it and the people in it broke me down. Then later, when I was too sick to work in the industry, I still had to do this strenuous work of healing, for society to see my efforts. Go to the right doctor, try all the treatments, medications, and supplements, spend every last dime and ounce of dignity I had to prove that I was trying to get better, constantly. Justifying that it wasn't all in my head, my pain was real, to be seen and witnessed in my experience and my dis-ease.

One of the biggest strides I made was when I realized that we heal in relationship to others. This concept is reiterated to me now through my understanding of trauma and the nervous system. I had always been *different, too much, too emotional, out there,* and whatever else I heard along the way, invalidating my energies and life experience. Folks around me just didn't get me. When I began to join women's circles, I walked into the room alone, but began to feel the company of others—the gift of being held and heard by others. As they witnessed my growth and mirrored my progress, I became inspired.

Seeing my growth and change through the eyes of others and how they, in turn, related to me was huge! This enabled me to understand I was visible, that I mattered, and that my energy levels affect those around me. I realized I wasn't alone at all, seeing others suffer and struggle as well, oftentimes in very similar ways to me.

Community has been a huge part of my healing. These relationships brought another influx of trust. I began to trust myself, energy, and support, and I understood how much power is in that trust. When folks told me I was intuitive, I started hearing that I genuinely helped them with some off-the-cuff comments I shared. My inner dialog shifted as well. With the uptick of nonviolent communication in my internal gabfests, I started believing in myself, my voice, my facilitation of energy for myself and others, and in my many varied abilities, including my ability to love and be love. Living from the heart space was a beautiful new idea to explore and extend through the essence of my being.

As I dove deeper into myself, I realized I wasn't alone, even when the room was empty of other humans. I discovered I had guides, always with me, always rooting for me, just like my highest self. As I opened my third eye and allowed my intuition to come alive, I began to receive messages and guidance from my spirit guides and those of others. I heard auspicious counseling offering me intelligence and loving words like none I had ever uttered to my own self before. *You are the pure expression of love.* This let me know without a doubt that this was not my own voice or arrogance. This is divine wisdom to help us navigate our human existence. I am poised to listen, relay and engage with this information for myself and humanity.

With spirit by my side, I decided I was done chasing the cure and wanted out of the health-uncare system. I began to build my toolbox. Not all at once, but slowly and with great intention and integration—a juicy box of provisions to utilize on my healing path. Reiki, meditation, and breathwork formed my foundational medicine, to which I added deeply penetrating frequency and sound healing. Herbalism found me busy and inspired with my hands in the dirt to grow and make my own medicines. My days began to include medicinal teas. My house and garden became adorned with crystals and stones that raised and shifted the vibrations around me. I investigated my astrology, human design, and enneagram to understand my uniqueness and begin working with my essence's grain. When I wasn't sure what was next or if I was still going the right way, I'd refer to oracle cards and divination using my own body and other tools. Learning my body's yes's, and no's and speaking to myself in this profound way unearthed my inner knowing and awakened a new rapport with myself.

Then, the tragic and sudden loss of my best friend, murdered, and my younger cousin, lost to suicide, took me deeper. I had uncontrollable somatic experiences leading me to investigate trauma and nervous system regulation, now my life's work. As I studied shamanism, I was shown how all along the way, I was implementing these principles into my life, my healing, and my tending to self, earth, and others. Each modality I've learned has been a step for me to go deeper within and synchronously to climb to my highest self.

Shifting perspective from fixing myself to being myself allowed me to stop working so hard to be sick or better. I moved my attention away from getting better, accepted that we are perfectly formed from birth, and focused instead on the feelings I wanted to experience in my body, mind, and soul. I went a step past the fix on to the feeling of being healthy, living a life, and seeing myself—my highest self—as true, worthy, whole, and good. That's not to say there wasn't a lot of screaming and crying along the way, itchy discomfort in the changes, and confusion in my newfound belief systems enabling this complete paradigm shift. I didn't know it then, but I was divinely guided to my true callings and utmost health. With the filling of my toolbox, I realized the profound effect of deeply nourishing myself on all levels. I saw the benefit of how asking others for help lifted them and me higher. It was symbiotic, encouraging me to create my business, LUMENous Healing LLC, to give back, and hold up the mirror for others, bursting through limiting beliefs and scarcity mindsets to find my new truth and help others do the same. Business as a spiritual journey101!

In the end, I didn't heal by jumping up and throwing my toolbox at every symptom each day. I healed because I began to allow, surrender, and let go of the outcome of every effort I put in place. I began to just be, relax into myself, stop pushing away what I really wanted, lean into myself and the unknown, and invite abundance in. It seems obvious. Trying so hard to do something I couldn't do wasn't working, so I turned it into something I could do. Using my many tools at this point, I showed up for myself with a greater capacity than I had ever experienced. Eventually, that grew into having such a great capacity that I can now share with others. I began to follow my intuition and natural impulses, which led me to a whole new life and back to my true self. This empowered action brought about a real shift away from the hopelessness and helplessness I was consumed by and surrounded me in vibes supporting my inner work and expansive growth.

As you're reading this chapter, you can start right now to make significant shifts in your life. Begin simply by paying close attention to your subtle self by tuning in. You can do this in several ways:

With a body scan—noticing your body parts from head to toe or reverse, their subtleties, where they make contact to your environment, the nuances of temperature and texture, etc.

With humming—feeling your unique frequency and vibration reverberate in the body, bringing you into tune with yourself.

By looking at or making contact with yourself—watching your body move, caressing its joints, appreciating every sensation and movement it experiences in a very slow, considered manner.

Go through your days with a different dialog with yourself and your body. Engage a childlike curiosity, asking yourself how it feels to do certain things or be with certain people or in certain places, emotionally and physically. Invest the time to sink in, listen to your whole self, notice how you move, how each body part affects the next, and realize the same is true of the energy you carry and send out around you.

We are waves—waves of energy, waves of human experience, waves of expression. Learn not just to ride these waves, but to examine and recognize them, feel them, peek into the barrel of their expression and notice how you are in response, in relation, and as one. In this deep tuning, you'll begin to hear your soul's whisper as it brings online the innate wisdom of your body. You will start to remember who you truly are, who you've always been. Your soul knows the way—just follow.

And to be clear, I'm not healed, and I'm not done healing. Healing itself is not the final destination; healing is never complete. This chapter is one of the ways in which I'm honoring my unique journey, recognizing my growth, and celebrating myself in my illuminated glory! It's one step. I'm on the path to becoming my most evolved self for today, ready to harvest the fruits of all my energetic labor. With my business and my health as my spirit guides, I'm honored to help others realize their innate power. Let's live fully embodied and fiercely empowered!

Kelbi is a multi-dimensional being currently residing on Muscogee Creek land in Georgia. She enjoys a cozy cup of tea, engaging conversation, a high vibrational crystal grid, and sitting by the lake and fire with her husband Sam and their daughter Lumen, whom her business LUMENous Healing is named. Born and raised in Florida, she has survived a climate of hurricanes in her body and lives to heal about it and help others do the same. Kelbi is a quantum energy facilitator, shamanic healer, reiki master, community herbalist, medicine grower and is passionate about healing trauma through nervous system regulation. When she's not elbow-deep in the dirt, you may find her daydreaming and journaling in the shade or inside, playing healing frequencies for herself and the medicine she's making. She is an ever-evolving healer for herself and others, consistently challenging herself to learn and understand energy and healing in new ways, adding to her list of modalities, amplifying her set of tools and services. Finding her way from chronic illness and complete disassociation and moving into embodiment, Kelbi has made transformational shifts in her life, and she aims to share these possibilities with others.

In Kelbi's Ambient Flow sessions, you may experience one or all of her talents: energy and chakra clearing/alignment, Reiki/Quantum/Auric Light/Etc practices, shamanic journeys/healing and soul retrieval, nervous system regulation, frequency/sound tuning, reaching a deeply relaxed, clear and ultimately healing theta state, channeled intuitive messages and light languages, drumming, and more. She works with humans, animals, places, births, and deaths. Be in touch to start to carve out your unique healing path.

Discover Kelbi, learn more, and connect on her website at
www.LUMENousHealing.com,
Instagram, and Facebook: @LUMENousHealing.
Healing services and garden located in Atlanta/Clarkston, Georgia,
remote services worldwide.

CHAPTER 14

CRASHING THROUGH THE PORTAL DOOR

Jordan O'Connor, BScN, Sacred Union Alchemist

I Can't Breathe!

I hear my own scream inside my mind.

I can't speak.

There is no air. I feel the hot tears burn my eyes, as my heart explodes inside of my chest. I feel the grip of panic instantly flood my body. My solar plexus turns inside out. The pain. The constriction. No air. My system closes down. Threatening to consume me.

I'm dying!

Again, the echo of my voice.

Screaming. Screaming inside. Screaming to save my life.

How long have I been screaming inside? I wonder.

The inquiry surprises me. I am drowning in eternity, yearning to breathe again. Trapped on the floor in an infinite now—a self-created Hell.

I have no control or space for response. There is no space for the bottomless shame and humiliation brewing underneath my terror. My survival reaction is in full flare.

How in the living fuck did I get here? How am I this woman on the floor? How is this happening?

Over two decades of personal and spiritual growth, facilitating, coaching, nursing, educated, prosperous, cultured, and well-traveled, yet here I am—on the floor, fearing for my life.

How long have I been screaming inside? How long have I been dying inside? How long have I been lying to myself?

Look up!

I hear a sharp blast—my own voice. Yet, not my voice, a command that blasts through my mind.

I look up. Way up. I see a crystalline avatar of infinite height and light.

Am I seeing my soul?

Is this the Angel of Death?

Is this the moment I've prayed for so many times?

Please! I want to live!

I hear myself plead to the deity before me. I long and ache to feel life fully again, to feel the air in my precious lungs.

Help me! I scream. *I'm dying!*

The avatar reaches down toward me, and I see it more clearly—a Divine being of light. I'm overcome with awe, unwavering peace, and serenity. The kitchen is gone. My body is gone. I feel a sense of safety, home and familiarity. I'm invited to look closer. I surrender and lean in. I open. I see that she is me.

In a flash, the divine being shows me all times and spaces. I am shown that I am all that is, and all that ever will be. I am shown my infinite multidimensional nature, and I see that I have never been alone on this path.

I am delivered a warm rush of love, and the calmness deepens. I am shown there is no death, but only the release of the human physicality as it returns to its organic nature—to the earth from whence it came.

I feel spacious and infinite. My body is then filled with a warm, soothing light. I feel completely at peace, as I am suspended outside of time and space. My heart leaps in bliss as I see clearly for the very first time.

Now I am instantly transported to the view of an eagle. My upward view from the floor suddenly spins, and I find myself looking down from a place on the ceiling. Have I died? Have I become an angel?

I become the avatar, looking over my collapsed and trapped body. I see the scene clearly. I am given new eyes to perceive the truth. I feel no fear, panic, judgment, victimization, or emotion. Yet I'm not indifferent, nor disassociated, but a powerful creator of my own story. This is a story of seeing and healing. I am shown that I am not nor have ever been a victim. My gifts are born from my wounds, as are yours.

The avatar shows me the soul dance. From the highest divine perspective, I am shown what is transpiring in this scene, this now. She shows me meaning beyond the violence and rage of two beings writhing in pain on the floor.

I am shown the trauma bond, the collective shadow, and the core wound in action on our planet at this time. The wound that pleads with humanity to be fully seen so it may be healed and transformed. I am shown our collective human suffering and pain that bleeds out of us and harms others through individualized fear, ego protection, and projection.

I see how I've been harmed and how I've harmed others. I see how I did not feel accepted nor loved exactly as I am, and also how acceptance and love need to come from myself before it can ever come from another.

I feel the avatar call me to trust, to let go, and to finally receive. To receive grace, compassion, wisdom, and deep understanding.

She shows me his pain. The pain I caused him. The gas I poured on the brittle timeline of our fate and the match I lit to create this outcome. She shows me all the ways I've done this before, in this, and many lifetimes. *I did this to myself.*

I see his entity, shadow, and localized pain-body fueled by the collective darkness. I see it feeding on my soul. I see myself feeding on his. I'm shown his soul fighting back against his inner demons, the inner demons that hide in every single one of us. I see his demons are mine, and mine are his— separate, yet unified, entangled. I see him writhe against himself, and I see myself in him. I am him.

My heart opens wider still as my multidimensional self sends me back into my body. I am once again staring upwards from the floor.

I soften, and soften deeper into awareness and compassion. I feel pure love. I relax. So does he, and his grip releases.

I breathe in life.

We collapse into tears in each other's arms. Relief sweeps my system, and I feel love. So much love. So much awareness. So much gratitude.

Happy Birthday. This is 44.

Six months later, I struggle to still pick myself up off the floor. I feel deep shame as I smile on the outside, dying on the inside. I struggle launching a new healing business, feeling completely off my divine path. I grope in the darkness, seeking the light. I'm barely strong enough to admit defeat and move on in life and love by Christmas.

My soul whispers its instruction that I must take for my ultimate liberation. I'm terrified of the mystery of the unknown—the only place where newness is born.

In a meditation one afternoon, I hear, *Go to Tulum.*

"Tulum?" I ask out loud. "Mexico? I can't even get to the fridge and back!"

I'm consumed in terror and have been paralyzed on the couch for almost two hours. I'm dying to pee, but the bathroom feels a million miles away. High levels of panic eventually exhaust me. I relinquish illusions of control and finally close my eyes and listen within. This is when I hear the voice for the first time in over six months.

In my surrender, she finally reaches me.

The next day in my meditation, I hear: *You are going to Tulum on the one two, zero one, two zero, two one.*

What the fuck. Then I put it together: 12/01/2021.

"But that's next Tuesday!" It was Thursday. I begin searching for airline tickets and a hotel. The prices begin to soar as the day progresses, heading into the weekend. The doubt takes over, and I collapse into overwhelm. Depression and despair settle in. I find my way back to the comfort zone of the couch. Two days go by.

Sunday night, a spark is lit, and I awake the next morning to the best gift of my life—anger. Anger is the gift that ignites action when we're frozen and dead on the ground.

I book my flight for 12/01/2021. I'm leaving for Mexico on a one-way ticket and have only 24 hours to pack. Feeling *more alive* than I have in years and charged with adrenaline, I pull out my suitcase. I grab my Canadian passport, sunglasses, and a few bikinis. The inner spark awakens, and I begin to feel the first glimmer of hope.

You are packing forever. The voice again.

"What? Are you fucking kidding me?" I shout to the empty space in the kitchen. "You couldn't have mentioned this while I was frozen on the couch for the first half of January?" I think I'm officially losing my mind.

Anger rises—deep, suppressed heat and rage. I rage at myself for all the times I never gave myself a voice, for all the bullshit circumstances I put myself through, for all the ways I morph myself to please others and not have my own back. I feel a deep self-loathing for the awareness of the extent of my self-abandonment. I feel the ache from the neglect of my weeping, bleeding, inner child.

Trust. Let go. I hear the voice say.

The familiar sense of warm calm rushes through my body—a sensation of deep and profound love. I feel a reassurance beyond words. I relax and feel the clarity.

I pick up my metaphorical crown from the floor where it lies dusty and tarnishing. It's bent and some jewels are missing, but there it is. A crown longing to be reclaimed. I bow my chin and feel the warm tears stream silently down my cheeks. I place my broken crown upon my weary head.

I surrender; please protect my heart. I am yours. I turn my life over to the Divine.

I arrive in Cancun, Mexico, exhausted, disheveled, and grateful less than twenty-four hours later. Hoping this is the end of a living hell, I discover that I'm only beginning my real healing journey.

For two weeks, I remain paralyzed, feeling trapped in panic in my hotel room. I cry every day and begin to purge the trapped trauma in my body. I have shrunk myself so small that I've *forgotten how to be human.* I'm afraid of everyone, and I slowly relearn how to live life without a mask on, physically and metaphorically.

Freedom is terror for the comfortable prisoner. But I grow strong, listening to my heart. I begin the long climb up the steps towards my palace.

When I finally make it to the beach in Tulum, my horror grows. I don't recognize the place I fell in love with in 2017. I see a stream of party-goers flocking to the many clubs and hotels built in greed and haste. I cry as I see the destruction of the sacred cenote land and shoreline that holds the waste of human overconsumption. I can hear the mangroves screaming.

I weep in the sand for two hours while the rain soaks my skin and blesses me at the same time. I let it all out, for myself, the land, my pain, and the pain of humanity.

Why am I here? This is not my home. What happened to Tulum?

I'm surrounded by seemingly pseudo-spiritual goddesses decorated in beads, playing crystal bowls, and losing their minds over cacao ceremonies. My stomach churns and grips in panic.

What in the flying fuck is happening here?

I ache for human connection and authenticity. My prayers are answered. I eventually find a few beautiful souls on a similar path for a time. Over the next six months, I move *fourteen* times. I realize I'm coming from a place of lack and desperation and am manifesting many colorful and valid reasons to keep on the run.

Ants, cockroaches, and leaking air conditioning units with buckets to catch the water. Then comes the breaking point of gunfire and murder only blocks away from where I am living. Yet the list goes on.

In March of 2020, Canada closes the international border, with only two days warning. I freeze.

You're packing forever. The voice reminds me.

The reactive terror is instantly soothed. I'm left feeling eerily calm considering the circumstances.

Go Deeper.

I straighten my crown and surrender further into the love guiding me. I feel my ego fighting for its own survival. It knows I'm killing it off through courageous action. It sees me coming for it. I'm hunting, and my weapon is Divine love.

I'm no longer controlled by my fears, doubts, shame, and subconscious programming. I renounce being held captive in a matrix of hell on Earth.

After feeling like an abused pinball in the Tulum arcade, I finally let myself explore other places to live in Mexico. I have to *let it go* to receive the miracles that want to find me.

I renew my faith in the mystery of the unknown. I begin to trust. I relax, and divine timing sends me a miracle. I'm handed an ocean view apartment at a reasonable cost, perfect air conditioning, no creatures, and a five-minute, safe walk to the beach. I am home. I move away from Tulum, with beautiful scars that bless me and mind-blowing stories of an incredible journey of resiliency.

In time, I find an inspiring community of beings on a similar path of deep inquiry and reverence for all of life. I learn to trust myself and others again. I reclaim lost aspects of myself and discover a beauty within that I've never seen before.

I'm given access to healing, divine visions, and deep levels of faith. I remember how to belly laugh and play. My inner child feels safe and happy. I cry openly and receive grace as the light returns to my eyes.

Tulum was not my home but merely a stepping stone on my journey to liberation. I continue to learn that *there is no arrival.* I learn to embody presence and enjoy every step of the adventure. When I finally stop grasping what my ego thinks is right for me and truly let go, I'm again swept into the flow and magic of life.

I take back my physical land space and claim a new home as I root myself in the loving arms of beloved Mexico. I take back my internal land space by commanding inner peace and radical self-acceptance for all of who I am.

I claim my divine birthright to adhere to the guidance and wisdom of my soul. I am held and protected in the heart of God.

This is 46.

Jordan O'Connor, BScN, Sacred Union Alchemist, was first born in Canada. In love with the beauty and adventure of life and travel, she feels blessed to have seen over 52 countries. She embraces life's various cultures, spiritual inquiry, and the myriad of ways humans choose to live and spend their time on sacred planet Earth. After spending over two decades serving as a registered nurse in the Canadian arctic, she now resides in beloved Mexico. Jordan has served women in their personal and spiritual transformation for over a decade. She is passionate about conscious evolution, liberation, and the awakening of humanity. Jordan now works and plays inside the Divine Quantum Field, where the magic of all life begins. Jordan guides the Divine Feminine home to themselves and supports couples who long for the creation of Divine Sacred Union.

You are invited to follow Jordan O'Connor on Instagram @jordanwjo.

CHAPTER 15

GRIT AND GRACE

UNPACKING FOR THE FUTURE

Jennifer Chavez

I admit we were already nervous as we drove to the clinic in downtown Lusaka. A couple of weeks earlier, we spotted that little blue line on a pregnancy test notifying us that we were becoming parents. I was never one of those women who *knew* I was destined to be a mom. After my non-traditional childhood, I wasn't sure if I had the right ingredients to raise children without losing too much of myself in the process. But that proverbial clock ticked louder and louder, parents were nagging, friends kept transitioning into parenthood, and there was the merciless itch of *I think I'd regret not at least trying?* This finally culminated in deciding to explore if parenting was in store for us. I got pregnant quickly, and so here we were, with that little blue line, understanding pretty much nothing about what the next nine months to 18+ years had in store.

The building was an unsuspecting health clinic frequented by expatriates for healthcare services from an American doctor and his team of reliable service providers. It was old, red brick, with low ceilings and long, busy hallways. They did a confirmatory test, and lo and behold, I was indeed pregnant, so I was sent to the radiologist for my first sonogram as they calculated that I was about ten weeks along. The doctor we were about to see was notorious in Zambia for his poor bedside manner. I was aware that much stronger women than I had come to him for his services and had all left in tears. My husband and I were steeled for the interaction and entered his room with a healthy level of anxiety. I entered the radiologist's quarters which were tidy but small. There was nothing in the room beside a metal examination table and an ultrasound machine he must have been using since the 1970s. I laid on the table, and he began the procedure.

After a few minutes of trying to figure out what kind of images he could see on the tiny, outdated sonogram screen:

Doc: "Twins in the family?"

Husband: "Oh shit."

Me: "Honey, take a picture of the look on my face right now because you're never going to see me shocked like this again."

Pause and silence from the doctor for a moment.

Doc: "There's a third."

Husband: "Shut the fuck up!"

Me: *Passes out cold for a few minutes.*

They'd ascertained that the third fetus was not viable by the time I'd come to. While it was painful to learn we'd lost one of our little souls, it was also true that on that day, we realized that nothing prepares you mentally for having twins than finding out it's not triplets! From there, fast forward through a pregnancy with its share of complications—but those stories are for another day and chapter altogether.

The first time my husband and I held our girls, we only had questions. Logistical questions were, of course, in abundance, but bigger questions as well: 'What kind of world do I want them living in' kind of questions, and 'if we can distill our life into a handful of lessons to share, what would they be?' Those kinds of questions. Even though we knew most of what would happen in their lives was out of our hands, we felt an incredible responsibility to shape their world and lay down guiding principles to set the stage. In those first days in the hospital, we took time between diaper changes, feedings, health checks, swaddling, and sleep training to discuss these questions and search for answers.

What principles would we select as the building blocks we lay for them? What from our past would we unpack to help breed the character and standards they would need to face their future?

In a life of more than four decades, I've had the opportunity to both build and be shaped by experiences and face and address professional and personal challenges all around the world, from Washington, DC to Bukavu, Kathmandu, and beyond. Through these relationships and understandings, I curated a set of principles that continue to test and guide my life. These experiences have built on each other to mold my adult self. What characteristics were keys to my success that would instill in our girls a passion for contributing to their broader community and creating their best possible world? I looked back at the moments and events that most stood out to define the woman I am today.

LOSS

When my oldest brother died, I was away at boarding school, a 13-year-old child 3,000 miles away from everything she knew and loved in this world. I flew home to spend some time with my family. I was mostly in shock and went through the motions during the services, knowing it would take a while for me to fully process what happened. "Be there for your parents. This is a very difficult time for them," people said repeatedly. I vowed to do my best. Three short days later, I was back on a plane to return to school in New Hampshire. No amount of begging my parents could keep me home so that we could heal together and find a way to live in this new reality. Instead, I accepted their decision, trying not to add burden and dilemma to their pain. I found my own way to keep facing the grief and eventual acceptance one day at a time, understanding the finality of my relationship with my eldest brother more and more as time passed.

20 years and two weeks later, I was on a plane again, heading home for the funeral of another brother. This time I was coming to Texas from my then-home in Africa to bury my closest brother and life-long best friend. My brain couldn't believe it when I answered the phone in the middle of the night to the sounds of my mother screaming what had happened. I kept thinking to myself that our family's tragedy was supposed to be in our past, and suddenly I was jolted into a realization that you don't have a tragedy quota or ceiling in this world. It continues to happen all around

us, anytime it pleases. The fear that comes with that awareness is real, and I'll be unpacking how to come to grips with that uncertainty for the rest of my life.

Being with Michael's body after his passing was an incredible part of my healing. From the experience of losing my other brother years back, I was keenly aware that these were my last chances to serve and honor him in the flesh. Perhaps his soul was no longer in this body, but my heart still felt so tethered to it. The only comfort and nourishment I could find in those days were in being by his side to help shepherd my family through this compounding tragedy. It was my last chance to make a memory with him, even if he was only the shell of the brother I knew and loved deep in my soul. I was trying to find a way to continue to live and breathe through the loss and equally with this fear and knowledge that so much can be taken from you in an instant, and there is absolutely nothing you can do to get it back. It's not fair, and simply devastating. There is no answer and nothing to say. It just is. So, we must accept it, even if we don't understand it, and find our way forward. Despite these losses, I got up and moved forward and considered each breath a little victory.

VULNERABILITY

In college, I applied to the Peace Corps and was assigned to serve a rural community in northern Cameroon. Over those years, there were countless lessons, including an acute awareness of my own fragility. I got sick so many times. I had one mysterious illness after the other, limited access to clean water, and even more limited access to proper healthcare for malaria, dysentery, draining abscesses, and other ailments. Through these continual bouts, my neighbors and friends from the village were **always** by my side, making sure I got the support I needed to quite literally survive at times. I had fever dreams about my death, and after each terrifying episode, they brought me food and boiled and filtered water from the creek. They would send their children daily to survey my strength until they knew I was solidly back on my feet.

Working at the local health facility, I saw these same inflictions hit the families around me day in and day out. While I'd given up the comfort of my home country to come and try to help this community, the essential learning I took from it was about their resourcefulness and commitment to live the best life possible, no matter what they've been given or not given in this world. We can't look at our own vulnerability and give up. Instead, we identify the tools and opportunities at our disposal, however meager they may seem to be, and put them to use to make the best of our situation. And our greatest resource is the people in our community. May we foster relationships that enable us to care for one another, no matter how foreign we may be to one another. In giving, we create the world we all need. In my vulnerability and surrendering to the experience, I became so much stronger. I learned I can, must, and will survive. My years as a Peace Corps volunteer fostered a sense of determination to overcome limitations, open-mindedness to keep learning from those who bring different assets to the table, respect for resourcefulness and innovation, and resilience to bounce back when life doesn't work out as planned.

FAILURE

A boss once said to me, "Mistakes are learning opportunities, have realistic responses to them." Failure is embarrassing, exhausting, and often painful. I've had my share of failure in relationships, aspirations, and professional endeavors, but I always heard that boss's voice in my head. *Mistakes are learning opportunities. Have realistic responses to them.* And those words have been a beacon in moments I'd broken things I knew could not be fixed.

A childhood friend reached out. He hit his rock bottom and was having suicidal ideation. He came very close on a few occasions and hadn't managed to go through with it. I was still trying to make sense of the raw grief of my brother's death, and now this was on my proverbial plate. What could I do? I spent hours connecting with him on a deeply intimate level and trying to convince him of his beauty and exceptionality in this world. I reached out to his family and asked them to step in and help guide him to safety. I spoke with professionals, seeking advice about what role I should play for him at this time. We thought we had some success and progress in moving him into a safer mental space.

But the night before he was to check in for treatment, he took his life. I was furious, terrified, heartbroken, and felt responsible. I couldn't believe we could get so close to saving him, and it had all fallen into an utter failure. I woke up to the news and was completely discombobulated.

I felt like I was in a million pieces and couldn't fathom recovering. But with time and deep thought and diligence, I came to realize my failure to save him was a different thing than his death being my fault. With that understanding, I could grant myself the forgiveness I needed. This was the only realistic response.

As I held these little babies in the first days of their life and unpacked all the love and joy and hope I had in my arms and heart, I saw that propping up my own satisfaction with my life to date was unexpectedly the **loss, vulnerability,** and **failure** I'd managed to see my way through. These darkest moments hadn't eliminated my ability to feel genuine happiness. If anything, they'd made these feelings richer and given them meaning I couldn't possibly have realized they would as the events were unfolding. I realized that the common threads woven through these formative experiences were the grit and grace I'd mustered in those times to keep going. These were the magic ingredients I wanted to impart on these little souls. Accessing grit and grace when I was out of control was ultimately how I became who I am.

With **grit,** I hoped our girls would be devoted to a cause and have the courage to continue to fight through the challenges that will almost certainly appear to block their route. Success takes work, sacrifice, and learning, and as barriers arise, persistence will get you where you need to go. With **grace,** may they be humble enough to know the value of living and working in partnership, strategic enough to make thought-filled decisions, and committed to creating a world that emits dignity and respect.

The early years of their lives have been magical as I watch them grow up with an intense kindness and joy in all things. We've been able to protect them as they approach the world with innocence and trust. Their agility was called upon when we moved from Zambia back to the USA a few years ago, and their resilience tested as they were torn from friends and routines and asked to stay home for over 18 months through COVID. As they grow and their eyes open to more of the injustices around them, I have the privilege of watching them decide what role they want to play in this world. I watch them muster the courage and energy to get up and join the fight against proposed transgender legislation in Texas, in awe of Ukrainians making the ultimate sacrifice for their country, paying tribute to RBG at the Supreme Court when she passed, and demonstrating for Black Lives Matter because, of course, they must. It's terrifying to witness their realization that the world is a far cry from the society we want it to be, but, as the guardrails come off, I accept that it's less and less my job to keep them cozy and safe and joyful all of the time. They, too, need to earn this gift of ultimate happiness by overcoming, practicing, and developing grit and grace to navigate tragedy and adversity and come out on the other end, still able to see the beauty.

 **Jennifer Chavez** has over 20 years of experience leading international assistance projects in the supply chain, HIV/AIDS, community development, and political transition initiatives around the globe. She has lived, traveled, and worked in over 50 countries focusing on Sub-Saharan Africa, including spending over ten years in Cameroon, Kenya, and Zambia. Ms. Chavez holds a B.S. degree from Northwestern University and an MSc in Public Health in Developing Countries from the London School of Hygiene and Tropical Medicine.

Being a part of this Sister Armor collaboration has given her the chance to step back from the daily routines of pandemic life and take an inventory of what matters most to her and her family. Joining strong women to share their personal medicine with the world has been inspiring in task and re-energizing to connect with others when the world has relied so heavily on isolation as a form of protection. She hopes that the time you spend sharing these stories will brighten your view of the world and remind you how many amazing humans and stories take place every day in this world. Yours is among them.

CHAPTER 16

ONE SIZE
NEVER FITS ALL

A JOURNEY OF SELF-DISCOVERY
LEADS TO PURPOSE

Jill Ann Brooks, CPA, Financial Empowerment Coach

PURPOSELESSNESS

I came out of the womb in an existential crisis. My mother came close to death during my birth, and I was separated from her while she recovered in the hospital. I bonded to my grandmother during those first precious weeks of life, only to have her leave me once my mother came home. I know I came into this lifetime with a heavy karmic load to resolve. My life was designed to be challenging enough, but coupled with this early traumatic birth and separation, I was off to a rocky start.

When I say I was in an existential crisis, I mean that I never felt safe in the world. I didn't understand the meaning of life and felt trapped in a place that didn't make sense. *Why am I here? What is the point of even being alive if we just return to the same place once we die?*

While other kids were excited to learn new tricks on their bikes or stay out past curfew, I was in non-stop distress, contemplating what would happen if gravity suddenly stopped working. *I wonder how long it would take for me to die while floating in outer space?* This particular conundrum kept me sleepless for months.

I was incredibly burdened at a young age with the need to be responsible to help my family, whom I sensed was on the verge of collapse. I was an intuitive child, and learned to read the room by sensing the subtle energy underlying our interactions, since the adults in my life were not forthcoming about the turmoil in our home. This was not unique to my family. I now understand that society withholds information it deems to be harmful to children under the guise of doing what is best for them, shielding them from the harsh realities of the grown-up world. But it had the opposite effect on me.

I knew that things were not as they appeared. I could feel it, sense it. "What's wrong, Mommy?" "Nothing. Everything is fine." Hearing everything was fine all the time, when my inner knowing was screaming that things were not fine, led to a cognitive dissonance within me. I couldn't reconcile what I was experiencing at home and at school with the things that I somehow knew. So, I turned on myself and disregarded my intuitive knowing. *If all these people say everything is okay, then I must be wrong. I can't trust myself. I must be going crazy.*

This started the many-decade belief that I was going crazy. Beliefs are powerful creatures, and thus going crazy can be a self-fulfilling prophecy.

I became an overachiever trying to find my place in the world. If I could just be good enough, maybe I would feel like I belong. My innate talents helped me succeed in areas like academics, where I skipped grades and graduated early from high school at 16. As a state-ranked swimmer and gymnast, I excelled at sports. I was accepted socially, a cheerleader with a circle of friends. From the outside, it looked like I had it all together. But inside, I was living in terror. The pressure I felt to achieve was overwhelming at times, and I started having panic attacks.

The first panic attack I can remember happened when I was six years old competing in the Georgia State Swimming Championships in backstroke. My parents had recently told me they were divorcing, so my need to be the perfect child was even greater. My memory of this event is still vivid:

I jump into the pool and feel the cool water engulf me. I curl my tiny hands around the metal starting block. *Here's my chance to show my parents how good I am. I must get a medal.* The starting gun fires its startling reverberation, and I push off the wall with full momentum. I frantically move my arms and legs as fast and as hard as I can, swimming the backstroke as I have done hundreds of times before. I hear screaming from the stands muffled by the water flowing in my ears and over my face. But something is different this time. I feel a weight on my chest that threatens to push me down to the bottom of the pool. *Why can't I breathe?* Something is suffocating me. My heart is beating so fast it might explode. I am overcome with tremendous fear that I am going to die. *What is wrong with me? I'm going to drown!*

Considering I had a panic attack (and didn't know what a panic attack was then), finishing fourth place was a miracle. Yet it wasn't good enough. *I failed. Everyone will be so disappointed in me.* But the more significant impact of that experience was knowing that my suspicion was confirmed by this strange and terrifying event: *I <u>am</u> crazy.*

These attacks became a normal part of my life. I still didn't know what they were. Mental health wasn't discussed openly when I was growing up. Keeping this deep dark secret was heavy. *I can't tell anyone, or they will send me away.* So, I hid it and stayed alone in my ongoing struggle.

I then started a lifelong obsession with finding ways to keep the anxiety, panic, and emotional pain at bay. I had no sense of self. I was desperately trying to fit into Western society's definition of a charmed life, because I didn't know who I was or what I wanted. I just wanted to outrun the fear.

Overachieve, climb the corporate ladder, make money, and have lots of material things. Check, check, check and check. But this lifestyle didn't bring me any solace because I was pushing myself in ways I was never designed to operate.

I never fit into the masculine-sacrifice-everything-to-achieve-world even though I tried very hard. Alcohol helped pacify me enough to keep on this trajectory for a while. *Why wasn't the American dream making me happy?* I felt broken and alone like I had not received the instruction manual everyone else had on how to live a happy, meaningful life. Fortunately, I avoided complete self-destruction when I hit bottom at 32 and got sober.

I made many mistakes trying to find my way in life, and hurt a lot of people. But the biggest mistake I ever made was not trusting my intuition, my inner knowing—the part of me connected to Source, my guiding light, my North Star.

FINDING PURPOSE:

I slowly started to question everything I thought was true, starting with religion. In my early 20s, I met with a Pastor of my childhood denomination. "I just can't believe innocent children born into an African tribe who have never been exposed to Christianity are doomed to hell because they have not accepted Jesus. How could a loving God ever bring a child into this world with no chance for redemption?" "There is a difference between fair and just. God is just but not always fair. God's will is not yours to question." This response was received by me about as well as the standard parental response when a child asks "Why?" of "Because I said so." I sensed that although he appeared confident, a small part of him had similar questions.

Something was shifting in me. There was a little voice deep inside of me that resurfaced. *You're not crazy. So much of the world you know is an illusion.* Could I hold space for the possibility that my inner knowing was revealing truths to me? Even if these directly contradicted what others told me was true?

I started to explore alternative forms of spirituality and divination tools. Runes, tarot cards, and pendulums held great appeal to me as ways to communicate with Spirit. I had found a much more open and expansive set of beliefs relating to God (Source, Universe, Spirit, all interchangeable in my vocabulary) in a 12-step program as it allowed me to create my own conception of a higher power. This was far different from the religious institutions that were a part of my childhood, where God was to be feared or be condemned for eternity. This opened the door for what was the beginning of an incredibly magical journey.

One by one, I began to unravel the threads of my former life. I tried on various forms of spirituality, even religion. I found parts of most of these systems resonated with me, but I did not fully fit within any of the boxes. The vast interconnected web of spiritual beliefs is expansive, with room for everyone. Unfortunately, man has taken these truths and warped them into fear-based ideology to control the masses.

I began to separate what I knew to be true from what I had been told or learned. This involved past life regression and remembering the journeys I had experienced before. We all have different paths to finding our truth, and different calls resonate for different people. I will never say my path is the right way for everyone. It's only the right path for me. One size never fits all.

I had to make peace with my body. I felt it had betrayed me. It had caused me so much anguish with the mental and emotional pain that was a part of my daily life. I finally realized that panic, anxiety, and depression were signals from my body and soul, trying to tell me I was on the wrong path. I needed to heal many parts of myself and change my lifestyle. But I hadn't listened to it. I continued to push myself until I had what the medical profession would call a nervous breakdown while the spiritual community would label the Dark Night of the Soul. I experienced several of these periods throughout my life. My body was screaming at me to make changes, and instead of listening, I dealt with it by dissociating from it, numbing out, or just flat out ignoring it. It was too painful and too loud. When I finally started listening, my entire world changed.

I found inspiration and a greater understanding of who I really am in Astrology and Human Design. It was comforting to know that there were blueprints for my life path. The instruction manual I had always sought did exist. The more I started embracing my individual life blueprint and the lessons my soul needed to learn in this lifetime, the more I felt the fragmented parts of me that I had rejected long ago as wrong or shameful return to me.

I found myself immersed in a whole new world of alternative spiritual beliefs and holistic healing modalities that were non-existent to me until I became open-minded enough to welcome them in. I became a Reiki Master, studied Quantum Psionics and Earth Energy Healing, and became certified in Feng Shui, Biophilic Design and Hypnotherapy, to name a few. My quest for spiritual information and learning the dynamics of energy was insatiable. I wanted to try it all!

Spirit led me to amazing healers and spiritual mentors when I was ready for them. This work gave me a renewed sense of purpose and hope in life as I started to heal. But I still held this newfound path very close to me and didn't talk about it with others beyond my spiritual communities. Another cognitive dissonance since my outer world (how I was showing up in life, especially in my career) and my inner world were not aligned. I needed to reinvent my outer world to align with the real me I was discovering.

The Universe constantly showed me signs that I was on the right track. A pivotal experience occurred the day I decided to leave Corporate America to become a spiritual entrepreneur. I was sitting in my corner 7th-floor office looking out the floor-to-ceiling windows. *Guides, I don't belong here anymore. I want to leave this career and start over, but I'm scared. Please send me a sign to give me the courage to do this.* It was then that two large hawks landed on the roof of the adjacent office ten feet from me. Their heads were pointed right at me, with their outstretched wings raised high into the air. I sat as still as I could, taking in their majestic presence, then said thank you and watched them fly off. I believe in and ask for signs from the Universe. These signs were my confirmation.

Within a year, I changed my entire life. I was building the life that I wanted, the one that would finally fulfill my Soul's longing for purpose. I followed the path Spirit laid out in front of me to make this happen, even when I could only see the next step and not the final destination. But I had faith.

I started having dreams of moving to the mountains. In my dreams, I was living in a house full of windows that overlooked magical forested mountains. I was in communion with the trees and nature spirits of the land. I was at peace. Mountains suddenly came into my awareness everywhere. I passed someone on the street with a t-shirt that had mountains on it. I turned on the TV randomly to find a skiing competition with the commentator talking about how beautiful the mountains were.

As if these signs weren't enough, we had recently visited a friend who lived in a beautiful mountain community in Northeast Georgia. My daughter proudly announced one day, "Mom! I found our mountain house!" My jaw dropped as I looked at the photos online and felt a giddy excitement throughout my body. "This is it! Let's go see it!" We called the listing realtor who said the prior contract had just fallen through so come now if we were interested. We fell in love with it immediately, but this was a huge life change. *Should we take the leap and move there?*

Later that day when I was driving, I stopped behind a car with a bumper sticker that had one word on it, my friend's last name in bold capital letters (and it's not a common last name). I have never seen a bumper sticker with that word on it before or since. My dreams, the excited goosebumps over my entire body, and these external signs from the Universe were my *triple yes,* prompting me to take action.

Today we live in that house I was dreaming of on acres of gorgeous land filled with an abundance of trees and wildlife in the mountains. As soon as I got clear on what I wanted, not what society says is good and right, or what anyone else wanted or expected from me, the minute I said "Yes!" to this expanded vision of my future, life took on a magical meaning and set in motion ripple effects where the next step was always waiting for me.

I left my career. I left my community. I left my 12-step program. I also left behind a relationship that was the most unconditionally loving and accepting relationship I had ever been a part of. But the mountains were where I needed to be. I couldn't explain it, and it didn't make sense to my logical brain, but in leaving these things, I found myself.

This *triple yes* I speak of is my North Star. This formula is inner experience + body messages + outer awareness. What I intuitively know, what I feel in my body, and what I see reflecting back at me from the Universe. If all of these are yeses, I have my answer. Sometimes I only receive one or two yeses, and that's fine too. It's not black and white, all or nothing. It's merely a starting point with which to dive into my truth about a situation, opportunity, or relationship. I listen for guidance from Spirit. I check into my body to feel a yes or a no (which are noticeably different sensations), and I stay in the present moment to observe the signs the Universe sends me in the outer world. It took me years of healing trauma and releasing repressed emotions from my body to trust this system, but now it's the only way I can live authentically.

Healing is a lifelong endeavor. Transformation is an ongoing process. I am fortunate to have found sacred practices and tools, the support of incredible spiritual mentors and friends, and unlimited assistance from the Spirit world to help me continue on this journey.

EMPOWERING OTHERS:

Helping empower others is now my life mission, to take the wisdom and knowledge accumulated over years of study and experience, as well as the gifts I uncovered along my journey of self-discovery and morph it into a body of work to help others who are on a path of transformation. I have found a sense of freedom and empowerment I never thought possible;

it is available to everyone interested in receiving it. Helping uplift brave women who are trudging forward against all odds on the road less traveled, the non-traditional path is my purpose and passion. Say yes to your inner wisdom and create your unique path. You don't have to do it alone. I am here to walk alongside you.

I have worked with many amazing healers, sponsors, and spiritual mentors over the last 20 years. Their counsel and assistance held me up during the darkest times in my healing journey. They dove into the depths of the mess with me, and it was only in my mess that I ultimately found my medicine. We all have a certain medicine to gift to the world. Have you found yours yet? There is no time to waste. The world is waiting for you.

Life is either a daring adventure or nothing at all.

~Helen Keller

Jill is a Certified Public Accountant (CPA) who has spent the last 25 years managing the accounting and finance functions for various companies in Corporate America. She has accumulated a wealth of experience and knowledge in accounting, audit, taxation, budgeting and reporting, new business start-up, and process creation, but her favorite part of her job was always coaching and mentoring her staff. She most recently held the role of Global Corporate Controller for a multinational billion-dollar corporation overseeing all accounting and taxation for eight companies with a global presence.

So how did she go from being a Global Corporate Controller to The Spiritual Accountress? She followed her intuition which led her down a path of self-discovery, and ultimately to uncover her gifts as a healer, coach, and channel of Divine inspiration.

As The Spiritual Accountress, her work primarily centers around helping women find personal and financial empowerment by combining her expertise in the fields of accounting and finance, coaching and mentoring, Human Design, Reiki, Hypnotherapy, Feng Shui, Quantum Psionics, and intuitive guidance to uncover and expand her client's innate magic. This partnership supports her clients on their healing journey, allowing them to find their power and passion, and inevitably their sacred wealth.

To learn more about her services and how she can help you become more financially intelligent and confident, and more empowered in life, visit her website at www.TheSpiritualAccountress.com or email her at jill.brooks@thespiritualaccountress.com.

CHAPTER 17

NEXT LEVEL BEING

BECOMING AWARE
THAT I WASN'T AWARE

Janice Pouch

As one of three daughters raised by a single mom, she learned a woman's place was wherever she wanted it to be—in the kitchen, office, or boardroom. This was all she knew growing up. She was raised during a time when women were independent, career-oriented income earners contributing to society and their households. She watched her mother, an immigrant to the United States, seamlessly pivot from housewife to breadwinner without missing a beat, leaning, of course, on other women in her family for support. What she didn't see was the grit and tenacity it took for her mother to safely change the course of the ship that was her family in a new direction after her parents divorced. And her mother did so against the wind and the current.

It all seemed so easy, so happenstance, without little to any effort at all from the perspective of her young age. What she didn't know about were the sacrifices her mother made for her and her sisters behind the scenes. It never seemed like they didn't have enough or they weren't good enough. Her mother embodied the belief that they could do anything they wanted to do and just had to work very hard at it—most times harder than everyone else. "Don't get distracted by people's opinions," her mother would tell her and her sisters. "Stay focused, smile, and push forward through obstacles toward your goals." Often this stoic philosophy, rather than spoken, was demonstrated through the quiet resilience in her daily life.

And so, she did just that into young adulthood. She stayed focused on achieving her career goals. She smiled and moved forward beyond the challenges, even when there were happenings she should have probably acknowledged or tended to taking place around her, for her, and to her. If it was a success, she smiled and pushed forward. If it was a failure, she smiled and pushed forward. Pushing forward through distraction, pain, pressure, and anything else presenting itself as a barrier was what she learned to do the best. This approach to living was a 24-hour, 365-day responsibility and required extreme amounts of energy. She was always busy, and working hard became a way of life—her daily practice.

While she was unaware of it at the time, she was also working hard to avoid her inner self, the ingestion of negative thoughts, words, and experiences throughout her past that seemed so inherently tied to the fact that she was a woman and a woman of color. She had become quite skilled at ignoring them as distractions, or so she thought. The result of years of pushing through the pain resulted in a stress fracture. The lack of internal self-care and awareness manifested itself physically. Every human being suffers some form of trauma at some point in life, leaving an imprint on the soul. Sometimes trauma is a necessary occurrence for a lesson to be learned or to place one back on the path towards their ultimate purpose. And while trauma is specific to every individual and their specific journey, it's not unique. Trauma itself is a shared experience—whether the individual acknowledges it or not. Trauma tends to be most problematic when it's not acknowledged and managed. She wasn't even aware that it existed.

Nevertheless, the mind controls the body, which controls the mind, and her body was speaking to her very loud and clear. One's natural response to pain is to seek medical attention. Over the course of two years and after several trips to a stream of doctors and specialists to solve the physical pain (gastroenterologist, cardiologists, physical therapists), there didn't seem to be just one answer or solution. One of her physicians recommended she pick up running again as a stress reliever. So instead of just running, she decided to run a marathon with the hopes of reducing her physical and mental stress.

Additionally, a marathon's daily training and preparation was yet another perfect task to avoid internal reflection. The less time she had to be still, the less likely she would have time to acknowledge her trauma. During her training, she experienced moments of freedom, accomplishment, and less emotional stress. While long-distance running kept her physically engaged, it did not leave much mental space outside of the training routine. However, the mind controls the body, which controls the mind. As a result of her training, she began to have physical pain. Some of this resulted from her inability to achieve the stretching needed for distance running, which eventually led her to her first yoga class. The mind controls the body, which controls the mind, which controls the body. Mind-body synchronicity— such a simple yet so powerful concept that was life-changing for her.

When I arrived at that first yoga class, I anticipated instruction on how to stretch to alleviate some of my pain. However, what I experienced was more than just physical healing. Flowing through the yoga positions of my beginner's Yoga Level-1 class came to be easier than I originally thought. Certainly, some positions were more challenging than others, but overall it felt quite natural to move my body in that way. The greater challenge came from the mental flow, meditation and centering, stillness, and breathing in a way I had not ever experienced. In so many ways, one's yoga practice can be an ironic metaphor for life.

For the first time, I experienced letting go and a releasing all of the thoughts in my head, the stresses, chatter, noise, and all of the to-do's. It felt like being wrapped in a warm blanket without ever having known I was cold.

As time went on, yoga became a natural part of my daily life. It became part of my daily practice. Over time, I began to improve my meditation practice, relying on it at varying points throughout my day outside of yoga classes. Not surprisingly, there was a significant decline in my physical ailments. I was becoming more aware of what my body needed physically to feel good while at the same time recognizing what my mind needed to feel good. This lasted for several years. As I progressed from beginner's yoga level one to yoga level two, Hatha, and then Ashtanga yoga, there continued to be a constant physical improvement. I was stronger physically, however, my level of meditation practice began to stall. I was becoming aware that there was more work to be done beyond the routine of meditating and yoga class.

There were some areas of my mental being that needed to be acknowledged, which would require my leveling up on my meditation practice as well.

This next level of being required a specific focus on restorative meditation and energy healing. The seeds planted within me as a child to avoid distraction by others, focus on achievement, smile and move forward in the face of challenges, spread their roots and began to ground me in a new way—likely the way my mother meant it. The level of mindful meditation I was on the cusp of discovering would allow me to acknowledge and eliminate distractions to center myself. It would teach me to focus on being fully present in every moment without expectation. And it allowed me to smile genuinely from the inside out as I move forward on my life's path.

The world of meditation has many forms and practices. For me, the practices of Reiki and healing through sound have proven most impactful to my sense of well-being. Under the guidance and instruction of Tiffany Marie, Body and Soul Connection, who has shepherded me through this latter stage of my leveling up, my first step was to acknowledge the trauma in my past—saying the negative words out loud that were rolling around in my head for a lifetime and chipping away at my peace (and my piece) of being. I was asked to then write on paper the names of those people from my past and present from whom those negative thoughts and beliefs of myself had originated and then light the paper on fire. Admittedly at first, it seemed silly to do, but wow! What a liberating and absolutely exhilarating experience! As if I had taken my first breath after being submerged underwater for a lifetime.

The next phase was to connect with the spirits, guides, and other benevolent beings from my past and present who had and continued to support me in my life. My loved ones now with me in spirit included my grandmother, mother, father, and a very good friend who on her death bed had me promise to live up to the true standard of the person I strived to be. These are my spirits and guides.

And there are the many loved ones still with me every day, outwardly expressing their positive energy, kindness, and support in various forms—these are my benevolent beings. You know who you are, and I thank you. One can open the passageways through sound healing and Reiki in order to tether these connections. If you've ever experienced Reiki, you know the divine effects of the practice. For several days after my initial

Reiki experience, I felt different. My body felt different, and my mind felt different. All of my senses were enhanced by this experience. From that moment on, I began to walk in this world with a new sense of awareness of my place in it. In some ways, my younger pre-yoga and pre-meditation self became completely unrecognizable. However, my memory of her inspires me to continue in my practice of daily meditation.

This life-long journey has led to a point where strengthening the connection between my present self and future self is paramount. Not surprisingly, this is an ever-present bond for every person. Through my practice, I've learned you cannot connect to your future self unless you connect to your past self. This process can be difficult and requires deep reflections on experiences you might otherwise want to push down and pretend don't exist. As difficult as this step may be, it's important, and essential to truly connect with who you're meant to be in this life—your life's purpose.

The practice of calming your mind allows you to connect with your inner self and acknowledge—and ultimately manage—any trauma. This level of tranquility opens the pathways for connectedness to your present being and bonds you to your future self, which is inherently positive. No step can be missed in this process. The knowledge and desire for understanding who we were and are and who we're meant to be also influence the way in which we engage with our inner self (i.e., the internal dialogue we have with ourselves) and therefore, others. With this in mind, each day is approached with the intention of elevating my level of being in every way.

Janice spent much of her childhood traveling the world as the daughter of a military family with Panamanian roots. Her love of travel, languages, and culture remained with her throughout her life and inspired her to obtain a bachelor's degree in international finance and a master's degree in Latin American Studies.

For several years, she worked on wall street in institutional sales and traded equities with some of the largest mutual and hedge funds in Spain, Germany, Switzerland, Brussels, Belgium, and Saudi Arabia.

After marrying and starting a family, Janice explored using her language skills as a Spanish teacher for several years and started an after-school language program for primary-aged students.

Ultimately, she decided to combine her fondness of people, experience in finance and education into a career in real estate. The bond she establishes with her clients enables her to advocate and negotiate effectively on their behalf while making one of the largest and sometimes most stressful purchases in life a joyous one. As a result, the relationships with her clients continue long after buying or selling their homes.

Janice is a wife, a mother of two daughters, enjoys traveling with her family and writing.

She is fluent in Spanish and proficient in French.

CHAPTER 18

ILLUMINATE

FUCK BEING PERFECT

Hayley Verney, ND Human Resource Management,
Certified Life Coach, Yoga Teacher

"Beyond the veil of the known, darkness and light intertwine together, in the unknown, waiting for something to be known."

Dear reader, do you ever feel stuck or in-between states of moving out of a situation or relationship that no longer works for you?

My story describes one of my journeys to the unknown during one of many life transitions that connected me deeper to my soul purpose. The unknown, the space between past and future, beyond all space and time, can be an uncomfortable and scary place while experiencing a life change, personal growth, or transformation.

Change is not linear in progression. Entering the unknown part of a transition is like arriving alone into the vastness of black space, like a space airport. There is nothing, you are nobody, there is no time, you are consciousness.

Now imagine as you arrive at this airport in space, a sign says: "Welcome to the place of endless possibilities."

You drop your baggage, the fear programs running in your mind, and choose an emotion you want to recalibrate with. I am resonating with hope, love, and joy.

Can manifesting, creating your future, really be this simple?

Standing in the kitchen, aggressively washing dishes with a lump in my throat, I turn around and lash out at my husband in a squeaky, emotional voice, "I am so confused, I don't know what to do. I just want out. My soul is sucked dry. I don't enjoy the political power plays, the egos in the boardroom, the backstabbing, and comparing whose dick is bigger!"

I observe my hubby's discomfort as he shifts his body weight and turns away from me to actively direct his energy into mashing a steaming bowl of boiled potatoes. We both stand in a heavy, uncomfortable silence as the steam evaporates into the ether between us. At this moment, I feel alone and can hear his unspoken concerns about my wanting to resign that he has raised during similar encounters in the past.

What about the financial implications? What lifestyle changes do we need to make? How will this influence our children? Will we make it work?

All the while, I'm thinking:

What additional pressure and stress will defer to my husband? Is it fair for me to create the work I love doing? Can I do the work I love? Is it a pipe dream? How many people do the work they love and get paid well for it?

On the one hand, it's inspiring and liberating to step away from a familiar past and let go of what no longer brings joy and meaning into my life. I'm empowered to make conscious choices and follow my heart. The future vision of healing and empowering others to become more self-aware and conscious of energy management magnetizes me like the moon's gravitational pull on the waves.

Why do I feel so heavy and tired? Should I resign from my job to be self-employed? Can I make it work this time? What if I can't make it work for me again? Is the timing right? I don't know what to do.

I'm experiencing dizziness from countless back-and-forth inner dialogue, and my neck is stiff from carrying the weight of the unknown on my shoulders. The empty and hollow sensations in my gut signal I'm out of alignment and operating mainly from my mental body; I'm disconnected from my physical body and feel anxious. I'm frozen, motionless, and stuck.

How do you know when it's time to change something in your life? Whether it's time to change jobs, let go of the apron strings, put boundaries in place, get married, start a family, go on retirement, buy a house or car, try a new approach, develop a new product, collaborate with a new partner, or find a new tribe?

Too often, we wait for something to break or for there to be a breakdown in a relationship before we change. In this situation, I was forced to change as I was retrenched before I resigned.

How are we sure things will work out for us when we have no certainty of our future? When I have no sight of the future, the voices of past experiences and conditioning start talking simultaneously. These voices of reason or fear are often from my parents, teachers, institutions, or those I'm in a relationship with. I recall a director I reported to saying to me, "If you don't make it in life before you are 40, you will never make it."

Who have you unconsciously permitted to shape your life, limit your potential, or silence you?

I have made friends with some of my thought patterns (beliefs/programs). As they say, "Keep your enemies close." I will introduce you to a couple of my friends throughout my story.

Self-awareness is my superhero friend who is an algorithm replacing fixed-mindset words with growth-mindset words. If you're unfamiliar with growth mindset, I recommend you read *Mindset: The New Psychology of Success* by Dr. Carol S. Dweck. Instead of saying "I don't know how" (fixed mindset), she suggests I replace it with "I can learn" (growth mindset).

My children mirror some of my pain; their life experiences have picked open wounds I was unaware of. This shows up as emotional suffering of not feeling capable. I recall teachers informing me that one of my children would never matriculate due to the extent of his dyslexia and ADHD (Attention Deficient Hyperactive Disorder).

Seated next to my 14-year-old son, attending his first high school parent-teacher meeting, his math teacher looked down at us with her beady eyes and flung his math book over the desk to us in a demeaning manner.

"His writing is appalling, his math is poor, and he will never make it."

I picked up the book and threw it back at her. "Don't project your views on us without understanding the context."

I've challenged many teachers. I am sure most of the teachers knew who Mrs. Verney was. I cringe at some of my reactions now. My intentions were good. However, I admit I was overprotective and oversensitive at times.

Thank goodness for alternative healers and therapists, providing us with a space to increase self-awareness without judgment. It's pleasing to see that there is greater awareness at schools now, more diversity to accommodate different learning styles. I dedicated ten years to teaching and tutoring my kids after working a full day. I was driven to show my children that with focused attention, strong will, motivation, and support, you can achieve what you want. This was also interwoven with fear of failure.

My friend, fear of failure deals a mean right-hand jab to my solar plexus. It winds me down, triggering weakness to my knees and allowing my ego to take control.

Would my children be able to deal with failure? Would I be able to deal with their failure?

Stepping into the unknown, whether it's writing an exam, saying no to someone you've never said no to before due to their influence and position of power, or transitioning into a new life phase like divorce or retirement, isn't easy. I think of the Ukrainian people at this time, as Russia invades their country. One can't imagine all the questions that cross their minds around their future as individuals, as a country of the world. Despite the fear, they fight with meaning and purpose for freedom and democracy, uniting them. There will be more about meaning later in my story.

Uncertainty shows up as self-doubt, lack of clarity, lack of self-trust, procrastination, and when I'm out of alignment with my truth or fearful of making a mistake or failing.

Self-doubt is the "wolf in sheep's clothing" kind of friend. We're in an intimate and co-dependent relationship which is somewhat toxic. She's hardwired into my belief system, mouths off automatically in the background, and requires no invitation to speak. She's manipulative and whispers from the shadows while I'm asleep (my subconscious). At times she feels so in my face and barges in abruptly, knocking her knuckles on my heart center and eardrums. She stops me in my tracks. She shows up when I think I'm not capable of doing something, when I do something new for the first time, when I know my insights may be different from others, or when I ignore my intuition.

Below are some tools and practices I use to navigate transitions in my life when I walk the tightrope between the known and unknown.

When I'm stuck in a fixed mindset and avoid committing to something out of fear, I shout out, "Fuck being perfect, I am capable!" Then I ask myself what information I need to gain more clarity, who I can ask for support, and what perfect looks like when learning something new?

Meditation is my armor; it empowers me to deal with the unknown. In times of uncertainty, I prepare a sacred space filled with candlelight, and I burn cedar wood, pine, and sandalwood fragrances to ground me.

Gently closing my eyes, I cocoon my body in a silver bubble of protection. I call on my dragon, Emre, to accompany me as I transcend beyond the known to the unseen in meditation. Emre's name just came to me; it means 'loving friend.'

Emre, my golden, emerald green dragon with her warm, brightly shining eyes, is always ready to explore the unknown. She's like a Boerboel puppy with powerful limbs who is curious, protective, and very loving.

I hop onto Emre's back. The fire in her belly automatically ignites my solar plexus, my self-confidence, and my will. I close my eyes as we take flight past the planets, past the moon, the sun, into the darkness, beyond the known. Emre is the fire in my belly and my wings as I take flight into my future. She's my intuition, backbone, and inner warrior, assures me I can let go of the familiar past, and I'm capable of creating from the space of the unknown.

My vulnerability of making the wrong choice transforms into wisdom and self-reliance. I stare deeply into the eyes of the unknown, feeling brave and bold.

Below are some self-reflective questions to create inner alignment when uncertainty raises its heavy head. Your emotions act as an internal guidance system, and joy is a higher vibrational energy.

"What brings joy and meaning into your life?"

"How does joy feel in your body?"

Some of my clients' responses are below:

"Joy is summer—It's like having summer within, even when it is winter out there. It's all about warmth, sun. It's also the internal version of eating ice cream or drinking your favorite cocktail on a warm day."

"Extreme joy feels like a gentle stroke over my body, like my body healing itself. Internally my body is pushing out all the toxins and replacing them with rose petal water."

"Joy is like an explosion; it erupts with a shriek, a belly laugh, a dance, or tears. I struggle to contain the joy in my body."

"Joy is lightness in my solar plexus. My stress and strain are gone. There is lightness in my step and a big smile on my dial."

I use joy as my guiding light. I make conscious choices based on what brings me joy. Sure, there are times I resonate with the denser emotions, such as fear or disappointment.

I light up when I can be of service to others, create sacred and safe spaces, shine a light into the darkness of their wounds, and empower them with tools and practices that enable emotional healing or mental clarity.

Joy immerses within in me seeing a client overcoming her fear of failure going into a yoga pose.

Joy for me is experiencing a client's realization of how their world changes through a mind shift, from feeling helpless and hopeless with no control over a situation to stepping into the use of their voice to create different conditions.

Joy for me is floating in silky-smooth, velvety waters of the Silvermine Dam, looking up at the smoky-gray sky with the full moon opposite the sun and appreciating the sun's light illuminating the moon. Both astral bodies are out in their fullness. Feeling my breath expand into my diaphragm, tinker down my arms into my fingertips, down my legs to my toes. At this moment, I'm interconnected and plugged into Mother Earth and Father Sky. Listening to the different bird songs, the barking dogs, the rustle of the leaves on the trees as they move. Joy is contentment and inner peace for me. It makes me feel illuminated like a full moon. The light and fullness expand from my physical body connecting to the unseen, the quantum field.

When your wounds cease to be a source of shame and become a source of healing, we have become wounded healers.

-Henri Nouwen

My experience with my children changed my path as I searched for techniques and self-regulation tools. Playing self-guided meditations in the evening helped calm their busy body and minds. Sitting staring at a candle flame for 15 minutes as an object meditation before studying improved their focused attention.

Aligning and activating their energy centers improved their performance on the sports field, confidence, and ability to concentrate on schoolwork. At times they would ask me to do the "crystal thing" before a rugby match, using a crystal pendulum to open, balance, and activate their energy centers. This is an energy management technique I learned from a metaphysical coaching course.

Nothing prepared me to deal with performance anxiety. Despite countless hours of study, they'd blank out in the exams and experience poor memory recall. The anxiety of the unknown or putting the wrong answer down would stress them out and trigger the self-doubt cycle inherited from me. Their grades would reinforce the "I am not capable," the resistance increased, and the pattern continued.

One of my life goals is to own and or collaborate with others to open a mindfulness school or implement a mindfulness program into schools and communities. I believe self-awareness and energy management are skills required for personal development and self-acceptance. Epigenetics proves that neural pathways can be rewired, resulting in mental, emotional, physical, and spiritual shifts.

Dear reader, you are responsible for how you show up in the world, for the energy you bring into a space. Space is where the unknown resides. Everything in the universe, seen and unseen, vibrates with different frequencies. Thoughts are electrical; emotions are electromagnetic. Light energy is wave and particle matter carrying information we receive as inspirations, dreams, thoughts, poems, books, and solutions.

The phases of the moon symbolize life's transitions. There are times we feel as if we're in the dark, don't have a complete vision of the future, or have a crescent of hope. This brings me to share how I use the moon cycles to heal and transform myself and others in my community. The moon represents our feelings, what is hidden—our shadows. I harvest the new and full moon energy through ritual, intention setting, yoga, and meditation. Many of my friends call me the "moon goddess," as I use the moon to radiate, guide, and heal.

I write this chapter connecting to the new moon energy in Pisces on 2 March 2022. It's a high vibrational, dreamy, creative energy. My intuition is heightened. I'm receiving light code and connecting to my inner wisdom. As part of my new moon ritual, I create a sacred space, light a candle, write down my intentions—things I want to create in my future. It's like planting vegetable seeds intended to harvest in six months. This ritual directs my attention. I ground my intention into the earth, nourish it with water and visualize it drifting off into the ether, pulsing past my house, past earth, the moon, and the stars into the field of possibility.

The full moon is a time to go within and reflect on what has been brought into fullness. It is with great excitement that *Sister Armor* intends to be published on the strawberry full moon, 16 April 2022 (or thereabouts). A beautiful example of how the manifestation cycle works for me.

The butterfly effect, known as the chaos theory, illuminates how everything is interconnected: that the flapping of butterfly wings can cause a tornado elsewhere in the world. Small changes in initial conditions can lead to bigger complex changes in a future state within a system. An example of this is the war between Russia and Ukraine. At this moment, one and a half million refugees have fled from Ukraine over the past seven days, supply and demand for resources and commodities worldwide are impacted. I hope you find many words in this book that inspire, transform, and heal you.

I trusted my intuition, stepped into the unknown, and synchronistically connected with a new tribe. This tribe consists of beautiful brave sisters, healers, and authors of *Find Your Voice, Save Your Life 3,* and *Sister Armor.* It's like *Chicken Soup For the Soul.* We speak the same language; spirit talks through us; there is no ego, just love, compassion, and understanding, supporting each other through unraveling and healing.

I leave this with you as parting words: Illuminate your path to your future self with what brings meaning and joy to you.

Don't hold your dreams back out of fear; you are capable. Fuck being perfect.

Hayley Verney, a professional and spiritual life coach, creates space for individuals and groups to evolve to higher states of consciousness. She facilitates the process that allows them to connect with their intuition, strength, and creative energy when they feel stuck or uncertain. As a meditation coach and yoga teacher with 20 years of experience leading people through change and uncertainty, she offers individuals a connection point to explore their inner landscape through conscious breathwork and movement. Organizing retreats and workshops is a passion of hers. Collaboration and working with a shared sense of interconnected community inspires her. She has an enquiring mind, needing to learn, evolve and grow constantly. This creates an alternative view that enriches any project or conversation. Hayley has been blessed with the gift of friendship, attracting new people into her life and providing a haven of support to those in need. When she's not engaging with clients, she can be found in her vegetable garden, walking her dogs in the mountains, strolling along the beachfront, chasing rainbows and the next sunrise, or dancing under the moonlight sipping margaritas. She has a powerful, serene presence and deep innate wisdom that facilitates healing through self-awareness and acceptance. Take inspired action, set yourself free and contact me for a free 30-minute introductory session.

Website: https://hayleyverney.com
Facebook: https://www.Facebook.com/HayleyVerney
Instagram: https://www.Instagram.com/HayleyVerney
LinkedIn: http: www.linkedin.com/in/hayley-verney-9613701b
Pinterest: https://www.pinterest.ca/hayleyverney

CHAPTER 19

TRUST THE PROCESS

JOURNEY OUT OF THE DARKNESS

Kimichelle Bain

Flashes of insight, when they arrive unbidden from the subconscious, often have the power to stun. This time was no different. It hit me hard when I suddenly realized the harsh and cruel words hurled at me by my ex-husband were a mere reflection of the way I spoke to myself.

Wow, I thought, *do I really talk to myself like that?* The answer was a resounding yes. Instinctively I knew this was one of those ground-shifting realizations that would change everything if I would only permit it to sink into my heart and mind. Clearly, the process had proceeded on without my approval. The insights were bubbling up to the surface whether I wanted them to or not.

I took a deep breath.

If I wanted to heal myself and move on, it would require inner change. Toleration would no longer be accepted here.

I should make that a sign and hang it on the mirror; I chuckled to myself. But it wasn't really that funny.

How I arrived at this conclusion, of course, has a backstory. And quite a bit of it isn't pretty.

The June morning sun shone brightly into our 15th-floor apartment. I felt at one with the sun after my beautiful prayer and meditation session. The feeling of being that close to God layered a sense of peace and calm in my soul. A smile came to my lips as I relished in the presence of Spirit all through my being. I remember thinking, *it's going to be a great day* while trying to ignore my husband angrily staring into his computer. After all, Saturday meant no work. I didn't want to be late to meet my sisters in the ministry program. My co-worker generously donated several pairs of pants. We asked some of the homeless men in our area what they needed rather than guessing what they wanted. I couldn't wait to see their faces when we showed up. Most of the pants were practically brand new.

Excitedly I put on my white outfit, which was part of our dress code. As usual, I was running late.

I'll grab some Starbucks on the way to pick up my sisters.

I couldn't wait to get out of there, and I hurried along as the atmosphere began to thicken in our apartment. I could feel his displeasure mounting as I frantically searched for my shoes.

"Where are you going? I thought you didn't have class this weekend," he said with more than a hint of irritation.

The look in his eye told me to hurry up. I could feel my joyful energy begin to dissipate.

Nope, not going to let him spoil my day.

I finished doing my hair.

If I leave now *I'll have just enough time to grab my coffee and pick up the girls.*

"Where are my keys?" I wondered aloud.

"Aren't you going to answer me?" he commanded. The familiar fear began to take hold of my stomach.

I already told you where I was going—one more example of how you never listen. Stop acting like my father.

The conversation rapidly careened downhill as my heartbeat accelerated wildly in response. These angry conversations, seemingly sparked by nothing, had become a mainstay in our home. Lately, I couldn't wait to get away from him.

Trying to placate him so I could get out didn't work that morning. He was *angry waiting to happen.* Although not much taller than me, I could feel his looming presence. Physically I was no match for him. Although sometimes an angry person myself, time had revealed that outshouting him proved to be an act of futility. I tried to choose my battles wisely. That didn't always work.

His yelling became louder as he realized I was trying to get out of the apartment.

What is he screaming about now? Clearly, my work isn't all that important to you.

For once, I wasn't really listening. I just wanted to get out of there. Fear began creeping towards my chest, which began to tighten the louder he yelled.

I have got to get out of here. Now.

All the words he was yelling became jumbled until he shouted, "And we should get a divorce." I froze.

By this time, we were in the kitchen. Stunned, I turned to face him. His breathing was labored, and I could feel the heat coming off his body.

What beautiful skin you have, I thought as I admired his arms and chest.

Then I looked into his eyes. They were alive with anger.

Shaken back to reality, I shouted back, "So you want a divorce?"

I spat that word out like so many women had before me, insulted by the prospect.

I thought we'd be able to work this out. Does he want a divorce?

This began one of his long rants about what was wrong with our relationship—me. Honestly, I had no time for this discussion now.

Even his timing is selfish. Can't he see I've got work to do?

My long and slow acceptance of his incapacity to engage in a dialogue with me had proven to be a painful journey. Today, I didn't have time to argue or listen to a monologue.

I have to go, dammit.

A divorce—who says that!

For a moment, I just stood there, trying to absorb what was happening. In my head, I thought I heard the crackle of ice breaking. A shiver went through my spine.

What time is it?

Barely breathing, I realized it was past time to go and began to inch my way toward the door. I grabbed my bag.

Aww crap, he's following me.

The angry words shooting out of his mouth tore into my back like bullets tearing flesh. Fear pumped through my veins, quickening each step. Experience taught me this would get worse before it got better.

My long white skirt swished as I turned to face him. My eyes grew wide as the sound of his booming voice pierced my ears. He put his arm on the door.

Oh my God, he's not going to let me out.

I don't remember what he was screaming, only that it was laced with the usual song of, "You, you, you, you." And not the *'wonderful you'* song, but the *'it's all your fault'* song. The impulse to flee overwhelmed my ability to think.

How the hell am I going to get out of here?

Can the neighbors hear us?

His spit hitting my face yanked me back into the moment.

God, he's too close.

I couldn't breathe.

He's about to ball up his fist and hit me right in my face.

What have I done?

He didn't hit me that day or any other day. I made it out of the apartment in time for my appointment. But our marriage careened rapidly downhill. That was the beginning of the end. As much as I loved him and wanted our marriage to work, irrevocable lines had been crossed. I didn't want to see how much further he was capable of going. My nervous system was already functioning on high, which led to sleepless nights and almost paralyzing anxiety.

The descent downhill continued for the following year. My ex moved out two months after that argument and many others. Although ministry school was a precious calling, philosophical differences led me to withdraw from the program. At the time, I hadn't factored in the consequences of losing my entire spiritual community. That arena no longer felt safe either and was a real loss.

The hits kept coming. Next, I was involved in a car accident that required hiring a lawyer and a court appearance. This added to my scary events list, especially as my emotional resources dwindled.

After my husband left, I moved quickly into a new apartment. The former apartment building sued me for two thousand dollars for not giving them 60 days notice. Fleeing in haste seemed crucial, as a fresh start seemed called for. My husband refused to file taxes with me so I could recover the money. Plus, the verbal insults kept popping up via email and phone messages. No longer able or willing to defend myself, I stopped answering him.

A few months later, two people in my circle of friends committed suicide, opening up old family wounds. Another family member passed shortly after. Although I had a few friends, the bulk of my support system still lived in New York. Being new in town, the stamina necessary to cultivate new friendships evaded me. The stench of failure and despair hovering around me didn't help. Even my relationship with God seemed dark. I knew God hadn't deserted me, but we weren't communicating too much these days. I felt completely and utterly alone.

Trying to make the slow crawl back to the land of the living constantly knocked the wind from my sails. Like a desperate sailor longing for home, each new wave threatened to capsize the boat dragging me to the depths below. There were days I longed for the calm well below the surface. It was all I could do to drag myself to the office. Nights were filled with pain and loneliness so vast I thought I'd die.

The journey back proved an arduous one. Everyone was wondering when I'd stop being so sad.

"Aren't you over your divorce yet?" people would inquire.

Unfortunately, I wasn't. How could I explain to people the end of my marriage was part of a painful mashup of circumstances too heavy to bear?

Unresolved grief and pain was my constant companion. Baffled by the turn of events, I retreated inwards to the mush that became my mind and heart.

What am I going to do?

I wasn't sure. Yet it began to dawn on me that I, for once, was not able to fix any of these situations. Time after time, they showed me that, no matter what I did, my best efforts were futile. That's when my fixer identity began to seriously crack.

Had I spent that much time trying to fix everything so I could feel safe?

What a painful question. For most my life, I powered my way through adverse circumstances. After all, I'd raised two sons as a working single mom, got them into college, and even went back to school myself after they left. The need to hold everything together was a huge part of my identity. It was where I learned to gain my self-worth. As long as I could do something for someone else, I was a valuable human being. And now there was nobody left to fix but me.

Did I really need fixing?

It was clear I was a hot mess but was I broken? Or had I always seen myself that way? This was another huge puzzle piece. And it made me sick to my stomach to think of all the energy I expended trying to shore up not only my life but the lives of others. Yes, I'm a good person, but this behavior blocked me from feeling unworthy and unwanted.

Was God trying to relay a message that it was no longer necessary to run away from those feelings? It wasn't my job to fix everything and everyone. Even my livelihood revolved around taking care of others.

It was time to stop doing what I called 'the pretzel dance.' This dance requires you to contort yourself in all sorts of uncomfortable positions in order to be all things to all people while neglecting your own needs. That dance showed up at work, in my marriage, and with my friends and family. No wonder I was so exhausted. It was time to stop.

What was obscured suddenly became crystal clear. My ex was a mirror for the shame and abuse I heaped upon my own head. My quest to be perfect as a hedge against rejection and abandonment had clearly failed. There was no one to blame here. We were two people in pain who didn't know how to cope. And the blame game is like a hot potato—and nobody wanted to get burned. Yet we both were seared in the aftermath.

To move on, I had to forgive him as well as myself for the harm done and for the mess we'd made. He was a mirror reflecting back the depth of my self-loathing and the harsh manner with which I still treated myself. That didn't excuse his behavior. The reality was that this was about me, and I learned a lot about myself through his reflection. A fresh start would require taking ownership of how I ended up here and where I wanted to go next. The time had come to trust the process of renewal which took time, effort, and support.

"What does that process entail?" you may ask.

I had to ask myself that first.

With renewed hope and optimism, I was anxious to begin. People told me my life was now a blank canvas on which I could put anything. That scared me even more. Who was I now, and what did I want?

The journey of taking my power back began that day. I realized it wasn't about what everyone else thought of me, it was how I thought about myself. There was certainly room for improvement in that category. Although I was taught to give my power away, the time had arrived to reclaim what was always mine. I could no longer use my power as a bargaining chip to gain security and love. Relief surged through my veins. At last, it was time to take a deeper look within my heart to begin healing and not rely on others and outside things.

Now I could stand in the sunlight with new self-worth. With a renewed capacity to open my heart to receive love, I could more easily accept my flaws. Love requires not only the ability to give, but also the capacity to receive.

This new venture was going to require a new level of support. Things had gotten too real, so this time would have to be different. It was time to allow someone to guide me through a new process of living from the truth inside my heart and soul. This would require a lot of trust, which was in short supply.

God works in mysterious ways, and this time was no different. Someone referred me to a therapist, and surprisingly we were a perfect fit. We instantly clicked, and our world views were similar. I needed that comfort. But the trust had to grow. After so much loss, I was still fragile.

Over time I began to love and trust myself again. The healing journey led me to new places and faces. I began to pursue a long-held dream of becoming a retreat leader and a certified life coach. Through school, I met new people and sharpened my skills. I saw the resiliency that brought me to this moment for the first time. Eagerly I kept putting one step in front of the other to rebuild my life.

The old ways were falling by the wayside. So were some of the people that didn't like the new me. With so much at stake, there was little room for pretense.

The journey also forced me to relinquish some old beliefs impeding my progress. The cost of entry into a new life opened my hand and released them to the Universe for transformation and healing. It was clear that the price I paid to see myself in a distorted mirror was far too high.

Although this road was challenging, it has not been without rewards. I have gained new trust and confidence in myself, translating to my deepening ability to truly connect with love and understand others. I know my value today.

My dream and passion for supporting other women on this road of healing continue to unfold. It's so gratifying to extend a helping hand to others. God has shown me grace with honesty and a renewed sense of purpose. I have learned that life is a process, and sometimes we don't know how to navigate those changes. But I know we all deserve joy and want to live out our dreams.

When life throws us huge transitions, sometimes the next step isn't so obvious. We all need a guide on the journey. It's okay not to go it alone.

Kimichelle Bain is a retreat and workshop leader, a certified life coach, and the founder of Kimichelle Coaching and Retreats. She helps women transition after major life-changing events like retirement, divorce, or becoming an empty nester, so they embrace the life they want without apology. She inspires her clients to be authentic, be courageous and defy expectations.

Kimichelle holds a bachelor's degree from Queens College and is a certified SoulCollage® Facilitator. She is a graduate of *Transforming Community: Leading Contemplative Prayer Groups and Retreats Program* at the Shalem Institute for Spiritual Development Institute in Washington, DC. Kimichelle has participated in personal development programs and retreats for over 30 years. She also loves music, dancing, and the beach.

You can reach Kimichelle at www.kimichelle.com.

On Facebook: Women Who Defy Expectations

Email: info@kimichelle.com

CHAPTER 20

YOU AREN'T BROKEN

FINDING THE WISE WARRIOR

Megan Crouch

*Healing is a beautiful journey of learning to love yourself.
It helps you let go of all the pieces that are not you
until all that remains is truth.*

Unbeknownst to me, my path started in college when I had the realization that I was a warrior in many prior lifetimes. My inner warrior longed to be expressed. So, I turned long-handled umbrellas into weapons, where I engaged in beautifully choreographed sword fights with my friends until the stem of my umbrella buckled under the strain and no longer served as a sword or umbrella. This impulse led me to take up Kung Fu training, which was the best and worst decision of my life.

It was the best decision because it turned me into an influential feminine leader who wasn't afraid to use her voice. My warrior spirit goes with me everywhere. I wasn't scared to ask hard questions or track down the information I needed in my corporate job. I dug deep into my inner warrior to square off against a bull-dick of a manager who was trying to break the spirit of my team because he couldn't understand what we did. After watching Amy Cuddy's Ted Talk on body language, one of my teammates and I set up early in the conference room where we would meet our manager.

With my legs and arms spread as wide as I could, I asked her, "Do you think this is enough space?" We giggled like schoolgirls as we practiced taking up space.

I love the potent energy that my warrior spirit holds.

It was the worst decision because the wounded side of my warrior energy forced me to extremes. At one point in my life, I worked out two to four hours a day, six days a week, plus working 40 to 50 hours a week and partying hard on the weekends with my friends. I broke my body down like a candle with a blowtorch on both ends. I frequently got sick during that time, but I'm stubborn. I forced myself through pain and discomfort. I continued to push myself to extremes until finally, my body had enough of me not listening to it, and it took me down for the count, forcing me to change my entire life to heal.

It would start with a metallic taste in my mouth like I licked the metallic zipper on my cheap Target hoodie. Then, my heart would begin to race as my stomach churned and my mouth filled with the bitter burn of tinny, sharp saliva. I knew it was only a matter of minutes. If I was out in public, I would politely excuse myself from the table to use the restroom as the first beads of sweat started to pool on my forehead. Then, I would quickly but calmly make my way to the bathroom, praying that no one else would be there.

If possible, I would search for a recently cleaned toilet, one where the lid was up, and you could faintly smell the remains of the cleaning solution. I would feel *lucky* if I found one. Clean or used, I would position myself carefully between the grey walls of the bathroom stall and the toilet, trying not to touch too much. *This is so gross.*

"Huuuurggehh!" and the dry vomiting would begin.

"Huuuurggehh! Huuuurggehh!" Then, my body and stomach would release and let go, which brought up the actual vomit.

Time seemed to simultaneously slow down and speed up as my body purged itself into the now not-so-clean toilet. The acrid stench of vomit would penetrate my nostrils as I prayed, *please don't let me touch anything. Please don't let me touch anything gross.*

When it was done, I would clean myself up, red-faced from the experience and the shame, and make my way back to wherever I was. At least one concerned friend would ask, "You okay?"

In return, I would nod my head and flash a weak smile as I fought back the tears. How do you explain to people that you have no fucking clue why you are losing control of your body? How do you go from being in excellent athletic shape to hugging a toilet bowl for moral support? How do you describe to someone what it's like to be stuck in traffic and having to swallow your own vomit, so you don't make a mess in your car? The vomiting went on for so long and got so intense that I developed minor bruises under my eyes every time I threw up. To this day, I cry when I throw up, so I do all that I can to avoid it.

Eventually, I was placed into a medically induced menopause for my last allopathic treatment to reset my hormones. I received a monthly shot for six months while still suffering from relentless vomiting. A month after the treatment ended, I threw up one more time in a small-town bookstore bathroom somewhere up north while on vacation with a friend.

That treatment was what I needed to start the actual healing process. However, I was still having issues with my cycle, so I started searching for alternative healers to help me fix what was wrong with me. Finally, things were better, but I felt broken and worthless. So, the next phase of my healing started, and it was more intense than the physical ailment.

I never wanted to have kids. At the young age of thirteen, I knew that I couldn't have kids. I have no idea where that thought came from, but I had it. Going through all of the issues with my hormones and ovaries was devastating. It is one thing to have the idea that you can't have kids, and it is another thing altogether to realize that the likelihood of you being able to have kids is slim.

That realization broke something in me. *What man would ever want me; I'm defective?* I was plagued with the thought that I was less of a woman because I no longer had a choice whether to have kids or not. Of course, I realize that nothing is wrong or unlovable about me. But that is where my journey started, looking for a destination cure to fix all that I felt was lost and broken within me.

A few months after that day in the bookstore, I started massage school. It was a dream that I'd had for at least seven years before going. It began with my martial arts training, and finally, because of my illness, I could now afford the school of my dreams without the social life to distract me. I immersed myself in the learning and healing process. I remember keeping people at such a distance because I felt so horrible about myself, and I hated my body for what it was still going through. There were connections, but I never fully allowed myself to connect on a deeper level. School and my recovery from my illness took me down two very distinct but eventually interconnected paths. One path was my spiritual healing, and the other was my leadership development.

Alternative healing methods gave me back my life more than the allopathic medicines doctors prescribed. Usually, the healers that made the most significant change in my life were educated first in conventional education or healing, who reached burnout or other life alternating situations. These healers balanced their healing modalities with life. One of the first Akashic Records readers was just such a person. She balanced her healing with her corporate job, much like my massage therapy practice and corporate career. She had such expertise and grace going into my book of life to access various past life information affecting my current life. She introduced me to other healers who helped me clear energetic blocks and taught me to keep the energy around me clear. This healing opened me to a new way of being in the world, and I loved it.

When I took my first Akashic Records reading class, I'm not sure what I expected. That's not true; I hoped for a life-altering experience that would prove to me that my true calling was as a healer like I knew in my heart. Instead, everyone around me seemed to be having the experience that I yearned for.

One classmate exclaimed, "Archangel Michael is here, and he's saying…" and another shared, "I see the Mother Mary…". They would then share the most impressive and in-depth accounts from the records.

One by one, those around me seemed to spring to life as Akashic Records readers—all of them except me. I looked around the beautiful living room where the class was being hosted with beads of sweat starting to form on my forehead, thinking to myself, *Fuck, I'm not seeing anything. C'mon, see damn it. Damn, my back is killing me. Why aren't the angels showing themselves to me? What's wrong with me? What am I noticing? Nothing—nothing at all. Why does my back hurt so much today?*

I so wanted to be perfect and effortless in my readings; I kept trying and went to one or two advanced classes, but it was more of the same thing. I felt like a failure and a fraud, so I put it on the back burner. Instead, I refocused on my corporate work and read everything I could about leadership and running a business. I read the *Strengths Finder 2.0* book by Tom Rath and took the exam to learn my top five strengths. When I read through the analysis, it was like reading journal entries of my life. I also continued to practice Akashic Record readings with limited success. I went to our local mind, body, spirit expos twice a year to explore different healers and tools, hoping to find someone to unlock my latent gifts. During one expo, I learned about *High Brain Living®*.

Immediately, I wanted to release stress and open myself to higher consciousness. My sister went with me to an additional demonstration; I was so intrigued that I signed up for two sessions to experience it for myself. After that, I signed up with the local facilitator for eight or ten sessions. Shortly before I signed up for those sessions, I became a team lead in my corporate job. I was doing my original work, my previous team lead's work, and learning the new processes and job responsibilities. To say that I was stressed was an understatement. I found *Higher Brain Living* at just the right time because a new manager made life miserable at work. Shifting my brain consciousness helped me navigate that whole experience and stand up for myself and my team. Although I never trained to become a Higher Brain facilitator, it would be a life-altering find.

The Higher Brain Living facilitator introduced me to Access Bars®. She wanted people to exchange with. Before I agreed to the training, I had a session with the Access Consciousness® facilitator; immediately, I had images of my mind's card catalog being cleared. I had never experienced anything like that before. I got off the table at the end of the session and said, "Whatever that experience was, I want to learn more." A couple of days later, I received the training, and my life would never be the same again.

During an Access Bars session, you hold various points on the head for at least five minutes to clear the energy. The energy would move through my body, sometimes moving me around in circles or side-to-side. Then, one day in the boredom of sitting there, my mind went quiet, and suddenly, I had a vision. When I shared what I saw with my client, they had a similar experience. I started exchanging with other Access practitioners and clients to expand my skills. I explored new ways to create a sacred container like the Akashic pathway prayer to learn what worked for me. I constantly shifted, researched, and tried new things. I had various successes, but I wasn't satisfied and felt I was missing a vital puzzle piece.

A few years after my vision started to open, I met Emily Joy Harris in the online world. My life expanded once again. Her healing was profound. I longed to work with her but also had some fears about saying "Yes!"

Finally, I did say yes to learning Quantum Field Work, and it was the best decision that I ever made. I learned so much from Emily about accessing the knowledge, distortions, and energies within the fields to clear and activate a person's energy. She helped me remove many blocks and distortions from my fields as I studied with her. After that, I started practicing with friends and massage clients. I still dealt with the fears that I might be wrong and struggled to get out of my head, but the Quantum Fields made so much sense to me. It gave me things to research and opened me to the world of Quantum Physics. I loved everything about it. It felt like home, yet I knew that I needed one more piece of the puzzle.

After reading *The Fields* by Lynne McTaggart, I started experimenting with timeline repair and how it could change people's lives. I had people write their past experiences and then rewrite them every day for a week. I then added Quantum Field Work into the program to anchor the change. However, the process was taking too long, so I started to figure out how to speed the process up when Emily posted that she would be a guest teacher in a timeline repair healing program.

It was the pandemic's start, and I was unhappy in my management position at work. I wanted something different in my life, so I signed up for the program. Initially, I thought this program would be something that would fit into my current work, but I loved the modalities. I loved having a structure and intention for each client session while allowing each client to have their own unique experience to create powerful transformations.

I learned that it wasn't about me or the modality; instead, it was about the client and their journey of self-discovery. I loved this work so much that I signed up to become a teacher.

During the teacher training, we learned a few new advanced modalities. One modality was the epitome of my journey. It collapsed timelines and gave clients the space to have their experiences while also guiding them with my awareness within the fields. Clients released patterns like procrastination, limiting money beliefs, and toxic relationship patterns. This work is deep and often gives me insight into who my clients were at their original soul signature. It helped me discover my own inner *wise warrior*. When we know our original blueprint, we know how we are meant to be in this lifetime.

We can drive ourselves mad striving for perfection and healing. Not because these are unattainable goals, but because we are already perfect and whole. Our perceived imperfections are the parts of ourselves that drive us towards self-mastery.

Allow your healing to be a journey and an unfolding of yourself. Peel back each layer, learning to love each emotion as you set yourself free from its attachment to you.

Sometimes we need guides, teachers, coaches, and mentors to help us, but the journey is ours. Find the healers who take you into the depths to help you remember who you are.

 **Megan Crouch** is the CEO of Sovereign Transformation, where she helps spiritual leaders and warriors release self-sabotaging patterns so they can step fully into their mission. She spent over 23 years in corporate settings, balancing her warrior training in Kung Fu and then her massage and spiritual work. As a result, she fully embodies her *wise warrior* energy.

Her daily mission is to help spiritual leaders and warriors release the triggers of the past that show up in their lives, relationships, and physical bodies. To be an influential leader and warrior, you must be willing to go deep into your healing to transform your life. Through the past, we find your future.

When Megan isn't working, she's connecting with friends and singing silly songs to her cat. She loves traveling cross country to explore new places. You'll find her somewhere in the mountains when the choice is up to her. One of her favorite trips was to Abiquiu, New Mexico, where she learned that she loved exploring nature but not sitting on a cactus. Her other passion is researching human design, quantum physics, universal laws, and alternative healing.

Connect with Megan:

On her website: https://www.sovereigntransformation.com
On Facebook: https://www.facebook.com/megan.crouch.56
On Instagram: https://www.instagram.com/sovereigntransformation/
On LinkedIn: https://www.linkedin.com/in/mcrouch/
In her Free Facebook Community, Quantum Healing by Megan Crouch: https://www.facebook.com/groups/quantumhealingmegan

CHAPTER 21

NOW WHAT?

A BROWN GIRL'S GUIDE
TO BREAKING FREE

Wendie Veloz, MSSW,
Reiki Practitioner, Social Impact Strategist

THAT TIME I LOST MY JOB

I sat in my Subaru Forester, in the parking space labeled Director of the Office of Policy and Planning. My throat was tight—I needed to GTFO of that damn parking spot.

I couldn't drive yet. I needed a moment to process what happened and breathe.

Stay calm. You don't need to lose your shit.

I felt like losing it, though. 22-year-old me would have been raging, furiously cursing while implicating everyone involved.

What the fuck am I going to do now?

I spent years perfecting my perfectionism so I could get out of the hood. I set goals for myself and went about crushing them. I nearly killed myself to be the first in my family to graduate from a university, earn an Ivy League graduate degree, and work my way to the C-suite.

I worked way too hard for this.

I had seen the writing on the wall for weeks. As usual, I was five steps ahead and had a plan.

Even so, I was back in the Subaru, still in the damn parking lot, looking in the mirror to see how bad the tears had jacked up my winged black eyeliner.

That Wednesday, I made sure to wear a badass black dress, pearls, and heels. Somehow, I secretly knew I'd be at war, so I might as well look fly rocking red lipstick.

My eyes in the mirror were puffy, and tears welled in each corner. However, my eyeliner was still solid. *Nice.*

I hadn't broken into full sob mode yet. That was progress since the time in my career when dealing with unsupportive and cruel bosses made me cry in supervision meetings.

I was in that same parking space, just an hour before, getting out of my car to walk to my top floor corner office overlooking the Galleria in Houston, Texas. I had a wicked view. I could see NRG Stadium, about five miles away, and everything in between.

My staff would come to my office to watch the traffic on 610 with me. Every day we were in awe of the number of people back on the road after the COVID-19 lockdown ended.

I started working in Public Health during the first weeks of the pandemic. I left my federal position in Washington DC, after thirteen years of building a policy career. I moved to Houston for this job and the opportunity to direct my own office.

There are very few Latinas in the policy world and even fewer in government leadership. I fought hard and often worked myself to exhaustion. I traveled the world, building my public health and policy skills. I earned that job.

When I walked into my office that day, I knew something was up. It had been building for weeks after the new Executive Director (ED) started. I began to see the same signs I'd witnessed every four years when working for the federal government during the administration changes.

The former regime's staff would leave before being escorted or forced out. Either way, the new folks made it very uncomfortable for the existing leadership and middle management. It doesn't always happen this way, but it's a nasty thing to witness when it does.

We broke ourselves for weeks trying to prove our worth. Did the new director really try to make it seem like we had done the wrong assignment? Did they seriously stop inviting me to meetings? I knew I hadn't imagined it; they'd been treating me like crap for weeks.

Every piece of excellent work my team did was criticized and shot down. Important meetings were going on without me and people noticed—I noticed.

My staff noticed. It hurt all of us, not just me. The difference was that I was a veteran of workplace mistreatment, so I knew what was happening.

That wasn't my first bullying experience while working in a government workplace. I faced similar maltreatment under the Trump administration, so I knew what it looked like when leaders lacked integrity.

The weeks before I broke free from my job passed dreadfully slow. Every time I woke up and left my dog Asha to go to work, it felt like being stabbed with a million ice daggers to my soul. I don't know which one of us looked sadder when I left in the morning.

It was horrible waking up every day and going to a place where I knew I'd be constantly criticized. Then suddenly the criticism and trickery stopped for a week, and it was eerily quiet.

Our department was the last of all the offices to present our portfolio in a 1:1 meeting with the new Executive Director. An hour before the meeting, HR sent a Microsoft Teams message saying I needed to come downstairs for an urgent meeting at the same time as my staff meeting.

"I can't. I'm booked with the team to do this ED meeting at 9 a.m."

The manager said "You can miss it; this is an important HR issue I need to speak to you about." The HR manager was a typical ex-oil good ol' boy Texas cis-gendered white guy.

I should have known something was up and started packing my stuff. However, I was confident in my work and my department. I had assembled a stellar team of policy experts with skillsets designed for a strong department focused on advocacy, equity, and performance management.

When I walked into HR, I saw a Latina woman I didn't recognize sitting next to our HR manager. He introduced her and then proceeded to the exact place I knew we would go.

"Your position has been eliminated. The Executive Director wants to go in a different direction, and your department is redundant with other departments. . ."

That's the gist of what he said. There was some other garbage in there, but I tuned it out because it wasn't relevant. He proceeded to tell me about benefits and a two-week period I could use to find another job within the county, but I'd have to use my vacation time to fund it.

"I'm not interested in working for this county any further, thanks," I confidently replied.

"Now, what are you going to do?" The lack of emotion on that man's face was frightening and smacked with toxic masculinity.

What am I gonna do? What the fuck am I not gonna do is a better question.

I didn't lose my shit. Composure won, and I responded with the sincerest look I could attempt.

"Remember when I started here, I had my own business on the side? I'm going to go do that." He had no clue I worked with a coach for four months and was planning to leave my position to be a full-time entrepreneur in the next year anyway.

"You'll have to leave now; we'll send your belongings to you." The HR manager said in a high-pitched whiny voice with a southern twang accompanied by an emotionless stare.

Was this man insane? I'm done with this place as of yesterday.

"No, I'll go get my things. I just moved offices a month ago. I have boxes, and I'd rather pack my own things, thanks." *There's no way I'm leaving here without my personal things.*

"We can't let you go back up there" *Confirmation, yes, this man is insane.*

"You're going to let me go get my things. It will take less than 15 minutes, and I'm ready to be done with this place, so trust me, it won't take long." I think he could tell I wasn't going to take no for an answer, and it would be easier to let me win than to have me escorted out.

Everyone in the room was uncomfortable. It was clear they thought I was the type of employee who would lose her composure. I couldn't tell if it was a normal procedure or if they thought I was a risk because I'm brown, and society views brown people as violent.

Again, they had no clue who they were dealing with. For years, I worked as one of the country's experts in addressing the mental health effects of mass shootings. If anyone wasn't going to harm a bunch of people, it was me.

The lady wheeled a cart for me upstairs and watched me as I packed my corner office. I opened every drawer and filled the boxes with my awards, books, decorative toys, and my ponytail palm in a teal-colored pot.

She rolled the cart down and took my badge. We loaded my car haphazardly with my entire office. I could see her in my rearview mirror, standing behind my car, waiting to make sure I got in.

That brings us full circle, to the parking lot and the moment I needed to breathe.

As I turned the Subaru key and started thinking about driving home, a million thoughts raced around like disorganized ants creating anxiety and chaos. I had to find a way to calm the noise and drive my ass home as quickly as possible.

Oh no. Home. How the hell am I going to pay for the nice but expensive apartment I just rented?

My plan still needed some work. I still needed some work. I wasn't mentally ready to start a business that day. However, that's what needed to happen.

I spent the final drive home from my office, letting thoughts run amuck. *First things first, I need to call my coach. After that, I'll go live on Instagram and share the news about my new business. Then I'll have plenty of time to cry and bury my face in Asha's soft blonde fur.*

I finally made it to my parking garage and pulled into a reserved spot on the first floor. I walked right into the maintenance men as I struggled to carry boxes into my apartment.

I'm sure they could tell something was wrong. My eyeliner did not survive the last mile of ugly crying. They had the "Oh shit" face men get when they aren't expecting to see a crying woman and don't know what to do.

"Can you help me take my things out of my car? I just lost my job, and I want to get inside."

"Yes! Sure, where are you parked." *These guys are angels.*

They unloaded the burdens I was carrying for miles and threw them into my foyer.

"Thanks so much."

"No problem." They walked out as quickly as possible.

I walked inside, said hi to the puppy, and started my new business.

BROWN GIRL'S GUIDE TO BREAKING FREE

Moving past life's challenges hits different for a woman of color. Upward mobility takes extra resilience, street and book smarts, and tenacity like a motherfucker.

We aren't encouraged to chase our dreams. Instead, we're fed self-doubt. We are forced to seek support wherever we can find it.

Being a brown woman is extra special sometimes. Especially when navigating a series of life's firsts like going to college, having a professional career, and healing generational trauma.

In the hardest moments when life's biggest challenges present themselves, the resilience that brown women show is built on years of uphill battles. Years of experience choosing to chase our dreams when no one believed in us but us.

Through the experience of losing my job, I realized that you couldn't lose something that isn't good for you.

LESSON #1: GIVING UP SOMETHING THAT ISN'T RIGHT FOR YOU ISN'T A CHALLENGE. IT'S A BLESSING.

Sometimes we hold onto things too long. We try to make them work because we're afraid of what our life will be like without that thing we're clinging to.

Relationships, jobs, titles, clothing, we hold on to a lot of unnecessary things. When you're a brown woman who fought hard for everything you have, giving up on anything can be difficult.

Now I realize that I didn't give up my career. I redefined how I allow myself to use my energy. I gave up my limiting beliefs about what success meant to me.

Success isn't a title, corner office, or labeled parking space. Success is walking away from something that no longer serves you with your head held high, a plan, and a smile because you know everything will be ok.

I knew that everything would be ok because the years of uphill battles have shown me that I will always be blessed.

LESSON #2: LOSING YOUR JOB ISN'T THE CUCUY (THE BOOGIE MAN).

From as early as I can remember, I understood everyone *must* have a job. Having a job was part of the adult thing. Having a job that you hated and paid you less than you were worth was also part of that job-adult-thing.

Single parenthood and underemployment have created generational money trauma for many brown families. It's easy to see how brown women struggle to create generational wealth and health given historical/systemic racism, trauma, and sexism.

Losing your job and subsequently not being able to find another one is one of the biggest fears many people have. This fear stems from our money trauma. It's hard for brown families to acquire wealth when they can't acquire enough savings to feel secure after losing a primary income source.

I was fortunate. I worked double time during the pandemic. Losing my job wasn't the end of the world. That's not a typical experience for everyone.

Not having a paycheck drop in your bank account every two weeks is the part that seems scary. If you grew up poor, the fear and money trauma from childhood likely created an anxiety button triggered when a paycheck doesn't come regularly.

Breaking free from the mentality that a job is the only way you can make money is the only way to understand that losing your job isn't the scariest thing in the world. A job does not equal security—you and your abilities equal security. Whether you choose to start your own business or get another job, you are the key to abundance. Not the job.

LESSON #3: YOU'RE ONLY AS POWERFUL AS THE PHOENIX RISING WITHIN.

One final lesson I learned from this pivot is that life is too short to do something every day that you don't love. Each of us has a gift, a set of talents that have the potential to change everything for someone else.

When we work in environments where our gifts are not welcomed, our talents are not harnessed, and our skills are not honed, we slowly wilt and die. We die in our chairs with bad posture and hip problems, wondering where our adulthood led us wrong. Unhappy that we spent so many years of our beautiful energy working in a manner that didn't suit us for someone else's mission that didn't serve us.

As a brown woman, it's a pain in the butt to own your energy fully. We're taught to be unseen, pull ourselves up by the imaginary bootstraps that we are born with, and fight but not too hard, or you might seem like a *crazy bitch*.

When you own your power, you must live as your core values guide you. You intuitively make decisions that fill your cup so you can go about filling others' cups.

I learned that my core value of integrity burns deep within me. I cannot do business with and refuse to work for anyone who lacks integrity ever again.

I can only step into my true purpose when helping others who come to their mission from a place of integrity. When I use my gifts to help the helpers who are trying to change the world, magical things happen. Ideas turn into miracles.

We're only as powerful as the phoenix who rises within us. As brown women, we've been burned, buried, resurrected, and ascended to higher heights many times throughout our lives.

Each of us makes choices that allow us to break free from the traditions, structures, traumas, histories, and environments that do not serve us. To do that, we have to endure the moments that require us to be burned and buried so we can ascend to the highest heights.

When we allow ourselves to stay buried, we let the chaos win. Our ideas go undone—the miracles we were meant to bring forward never surface.

As a generation of women fighting to do all the firsts, sometimes all you need is a moment to breathe, be blessed, be badass, and keep your power burning within.

Love and blessings to all my little brown girls who are chasing their dreams but are too afraid to get them. This story was for you.

Wendie Veloz is a coach, consultant, and social impact strategist. She helps social entrepreneurs change the world by turning their passion and ideas into sustainable businesses and non-profit organizations.

Wendie uses her 15 years of experience in policy and grant management to assist social ventures with infrastructure development. Wendie has extensive experience in the federal government and has served all types of organizations, including state, local, non-profit, and social businesses. Wendie has a deep passion for changing how community members and service systems interact by establishing partnerships, measuring success, and leveraging funding for a sustainable future.

Wendie combines wellness, healing practices, and skill-building into her coaching and courses to holistically support her clients. This foundation is designed for helpers on a mission to serve others. Wendie helps her clients avoid burnout by infusing various healing modalities in her work, including Reiki, crystal healing, and sound healing.

As a speaker and subject-matter expert, Wendie shares her perspectives on social change, entrepreneurship, and the importance of prevention. Wendie is also the host of the *Social Impact Level Up Podcast* and hosts weekly meetings with her Collective via the Clubhouse app.

Wendie is the founder of Wellness Grind, an online community for wellness motivation and accountability. She is also the CEO/founder of Wendie Veloz Enterprises specializing in consulting for social impact ventures.

When Wendie isn't gallivanting around the world traveling and living her nomadic life, she enjoys working out, international travel, and teaching indoor-cycle. Wendie is also a proud dog mom to her rescue lab-mix, Asha.

Connect with Wendie Veloz for coaching, consulting, or healing on:

Website: www.wendieveloz.com
Instagram: www.instagram.com/wendieveloz
Email: info@wendieveloz.com

CHAPTER 22

PARDON OUR PROGRESS

SISTERS AND SHAMANS
FAILING EACH OTHER
AND GROWING INTO OUR LIGHT

Jen Bates

I have always yearned for a sister. Growing up an only child, I would spend loads of time alone—well, kind of. I could often be heard talking to myself while playing in the backyard. But I was actually in deep conversation with multidimensional allies learning how the Earth worked.

There were secrets. For instance, I learned we have a limited perception of colors. They are actually light energy dancing, much like the fairy world I was so familiar with. I later learned this was in line with the ideas of quantum physics, but as a child, it was just play for me.

I would often play with Cassandra, or Sandy as I called her. It was the 80s, and I was a typical middle-class suburban girl longing for Farrah Fawcett's hair and real wings. I would ride my bike down the big hill in front of my house, and Sandy would charge next to me on her unicorn, of course! Her gorgeous auburn curls unfurled behind her as she glided alongside me in flight through dappled sunbeams. Sometimes she would come to me dressed as a fairy princess of sorts, dazzling in a purple gown with poofy sleeves and infinite sparkles. Other times she appeared dressed in the style of the day: jeans rolled up and a bit frayed, jelly shoes and a rad hairstyle with spikes and orange tints. She worked with me and always made an effort to shape her appearance so that together we could create a wonderful time and memory. She was a magical friend whom no one else could see, and yet, it never really occurred to me that only I could see her.

I sensed the lightness of her being and knew there was something extraordinary about her, but because no one ever spoke of her and she was always around, I assumed that's just how it worked. It's so funny to think about now how I just allowed things to be as they were; no need for me to get in my head about it or be stressed.

Perhaps this is what Jesus was speaking of when he said we must be like children to experience the Kingdom of Heaven. Sandy and I would be together all day, every day. All I had to do was direct my attention toward her, and she was available in an instant.

Together we would sit under the dining room table, and she would tell me stories about the multiverse and different dimensions of time. She was my best friend and the only one who understood me. When I went to school and became inundated with the energy of the other children and the teachers, Sandy was not as present for me. I sensed she was still there, but my attention was focused on learning and being well received in the classroom.

As I grew into a teen, I had no time or mental capacity to experience the magical awareness of my childhood. It wasn't until the entire world shut down in fear during 2020 that I began to remember Sandy, and she returned fully to my consciousness as part of my guidance team.

For me, the year 2020 was one of the, if not the very, best years of my life. I know, don't tell anybody, right? In August of that year, what can best be described as frequencies of light began to pour in. I communed with angels, ascended masters, dragons, fairies, and even mantis beings. Instantaneously, the world flipped upside down for me, and I saw, felt, and knew through my own gnosis that nothing was as it seemed and that my schooling and programming were ill-informed on many levels.

What began to arise for me was a much deeper and more expansive inner awareness and knowing—one that allowed me to be more fully in my resonance and ultimately more fully myself. Everything about myself that I had identified as true turned out to be just a small reflection of who I was fully and what I was to experience on Earth.

I immediately started searching for other souls who could connect with me in these deeper ways. I yearned to fine tune these newly discovered frequencies and open up more fully to them. Admittedly, my life had always been a bit lonely, possibly because of the lonely only child syndrome we hear about. I felt like I didn't belong with any one group or community, so finding one now seemed daunting and unattainable.

I had loved the world and community of the theater arts, comedy, and media, but still, it never really felt like my true home. I was the ultimate misfit and feared I might forever be alone.

I shared my experiences with Frank, my beloved husband, and found an embrace and openness without which I would never have survived. He listened deeply and offered all of the support and encouragement anyone would crave in a time like that. In August of 2020, we sat on the couch and I shared my experiences. "Babe, I need you to hear me on this. I know it all sounds so incredible, but please know every bit of this is true for me." I spoke softly while we held hands and tears streamed down my face. Frank reached up and brushed the tears away, his blue eyes gleaming with serene understanding. "I am right here with you, my love," he gently spoke. "I believe in you and what you say. Something is shifting, I can feel it too. I'm grateful we have each other as we navigate through it." Even though he didn't have similar experiences, he did feel deeply that something enormous was happening in the world and supported me on my path. Frank is the most amazing person I've ever known for his bravery, compassion, and deep intelligence. If you ever are lucky enough to meet him, prepare for a treat!

I longed to find others who knew what I was going through. I couldn't believe I was the only one. I scoured the internet and thankfully found a few who were speaking about this level of awareness. There were conversations surrounding multidimensional experiences and profundity of the times we were in. Their messages were like a salve for my soul and propelled me to find others on a local level for in-person connections. I yearned to find other misfits and to traverse this new path with a collective of humans ready to face it all with open hearts and minds. Soon I was divinely led to a group of shamans who worked collectively and were about to embark on another year-long journey of learning shaman tools in-person. I was over the moon excited and signed up immediately!

"Everyone in this room is vaccinated, right?" The leader's voice was agitated. Her blue eyes looked around the room with accusation and inquisition. This was not the question I was expecting from the teacher of the shamans. It was our second class, and I suddenly found myself somewhat out of body. A huge lump of fire rose from my belly and landed in my throat as the familiar blanket of shame melted over me. I pretended I had to go to the bathroom and somehow lifted myself from the couch I had been sitting on and out of the room. I don't think anyone noticed that I didn't answer her question. I hoped not.

I found a room to hide in and waited as the tears streamed down my face. Suddenly, someone locked the bathroom door, so I scrambled to another open door at the bottom of the stairs, gathering myself as best I could. Wow! I did not expect to have such a reaction. I knew this day would come, where I would have to say out loud my current vaccination status (even though this felt like an invasion of privacy, but what even is privacy now in 2022?). It surprised me that it was so soon and in a public call-out. I did not expect to have literal tears even with my heightened sensitivity! I stood frozen in the corner of a dark room that must have been used for some kind of healing practice and contemplated lying on the massage table. I'm sure it would have been a riot if a fellow wanna-be shaman walked in to find me laid out in the dark room, rinsing out my tears.

The assistant teacher of the class came through the room where I stood weeping. "Excuse me, I need to speak with you about something," I whispered. Seeing my emotional vulnerability, she responded kindly, "Absolutely. I'm so sorry you're upset. How can I help?". "I'm not vaccinated," I replied. "Okay," she said, somewhat confused. "The only reason it could be a problem is if the pregnant woman has an issue with it." "I'll go ask her," she said, and quickly left the room before I could say anything to the contrary. So, there I stood, with my involvement in a shaman course on sacred medicine of the natural elements and miraculous healing tools resting on the fears of a pregnant woman whom I had never meant. What a strange world it had become!

Eventually, it was decided that I could only participate in the shaman healing course if I wore a mask. For them, a mask in a shaman course was safe. It was obvious to me then that this was not the community I was looking for. A refund was initiated, and I said goodbye.

Why had I felt so ashamed? I had every right to make this choice and decline the experimental shots. Even my doctor had advised that I wait. Having recovered completely from Hashimoto's thyroiditis, a complex autoimmune disease, there was no need to throw another potential wrench into the workings of my physical body. Plus, I had already had Covid (whatever that was), so my antibodies should have been strong enough to stave off the next wave of invisible attackers, and assuage the fears from my circle of attuned seers.

Still, I felt tethered to what the collective was deciding. Somehow we were now all responsible for each other. Yet, as a mother of two, I learned early on that we can only control the bodies God has given us. I had not been able to go to the yoga studio in months; my beloved teachers had forgotten about me. Fearing for their lives, they had made the rash decision to require vaccination of everyone in the studio. Oddly, I never really felt the familiar loneliness during this particular time, but I did feel like everything was reorienting.

I began connecting with a growing collective of people who were opting out of the pharma experiment; this had been my main source of support as the new level of control was placed on our freedoms. This group felt strongly that what we were witnessing across the world stage—masking our children, confining people in isolation, not allowing loved ones to be together in their final days—these were indeed crimes against humanity.

Clinging to man-made protocols and hierarchical medicine for a sense of order was nothing new to me. I had been born into this world at a time when life's sacred strength and tenacity had been reduced to microwaveable dinners as acceptable nutrition, and Clorox-scented rooms as a determinant of cleanliness.

On the day I was born, there was a tornado in Atlanta. It was March, and Spring was beginning to show her abundant blessings, along with her fury—apparently. Mom tells the story best—the doctors said her narrow hips wouldn't allow me to be born vaginally, so I was to be delivered by C-section. When they arrived, she was wheeled off to a "special" corner of the basement. After being taken from the womb into my birth, I was immediately carted off. My dad was not allowed in the room, and neither were my mom's dear friends and family.

As mom was being sewn up, the doctor described his golf game to the attending nurses. She was basically ignored while she laid in a sterile windowless cement room, completely alone. Magical, right? Perfect for the witchy, multi-dimensional person I would become. Even though her beloved family could not visit her, the cleaning person was allowed in. So, the linoleum floors sparkled—thank goodness! Haha.

Forty-five years after my birth, how was I to assimilate all these newfound skills of multi-sensory awareness I had been developing? How could I trust what I was experiencing through subtle awareness when the world seemed so focused on physical protection and medical treatments? I knew in my deepest self that I was safe, and yet the world was telling me the only way to stay safe was to put a flimsy cloth over my mouth and take an injection from a pharmaceutical company. Even amongst those that claimed to trust in the natural world order, there was a program of doubt suppressing the very tenets that had brought us together. It was a bit insane, and I couldn't make sense of any of it.

One of the first resonances I had during the multidimensional frequency experiences was that of what is true and what is fear. There is a resonance with the trueness of life. You can feel it in the natural world. It's a homing beacon that we are all attracted to innately; it offers intelligence and comfort of what is so and what can never be controlled. Forest-bathers speak of it, as do many of the indigenous tribes. It is the wisdom and hum of the natural world and feels most like what we call love. We get distracted from it, though, given all the stories we are running, the noises we become accustomed to, and the screens of delusion. We then no longer trust what we were always meant to cherish. We start to only trust what our bodies can physically see and hear and what our minds can process. We forget the incredible ability we have to connect to something higher and more profound.

I have been shown that the sacredness of this frequency is returning to humanity now. It's connecting us to divinity and igniting our light bodies. The guidance shows me how our light bodies resonate from the mitochondria of every single cell in our bodies. We are so much more than we have claimed up until now. The land offers this rhythmic and coherent truth, and I believe we are returning to this remembrance now.

As we continue to create new lives for ourselves and gather together people who are ready to shake free from fear and control, we open ourselves up to this larger inner and expansive knowing. Together, we ignite a light so bright nothing can distract from it. It is why community and sisterhood are so vital in these times. Together, we will expand this tsunami of light until it is our primary motivation for all of the creations of humankind.

I am so grateful for the shaman community and all they have helped me know about myself and my own fears. We, together, are walking each other home. Each of us is serving an important role in these times, and it is through the friction and tumultuousness we learn our abundant power and inner fortitude. We are in service now and always to a greater understanding and an inner expansion.

I'd like to offer that when you find yourself gripping and struggling to find meaning; when your mind is racing, and you are lost in the thoughts and overwhelmed; not knowing how you are going to get through the next moment—that is when the best medicine is to s-l-o-w--w-a-y—d-o-w-n. Take no action. Cultivate stillness. Breathe into this present moment. Feel with awareness what is happening in your body. Allow the emotions to process as they need to. Remember the hum of the natural world and allow that medicine to guide you.

Maybe you need to just sit and feel the fear? Maybe you need to journal and bring language to your truth? Or maybe you just need to return to the ultimate healing already within you? It was gifted to you on the day you were born, and as you continue to walk this path, your experiences will ignite the truth of what has always been. You will remember who you really are—the light of you that is in partnership with the world collective, for now, and for always, and even all the ways.

Jen Bates is a light medicine intuitive and Reiki Master skilled in clairvoyance, clairaudience, light body attunement, and mediumship communication. Founder and creator of LightenUp with Jen Bates, Jen offers one-on-one high-resonance sessions to ignite your light body and transform stagnant energy with curiosity, compassion, and joy. Jen holds a BA in Theater Arts and Performance from The University of Georgia, and prior to launching LightenUp, performed stand-up comedy at many local and regional clubs. Most days, she can be found cracking up with her family, dancing with her dog, and immersing herself in the wonders of Quantum Consciousness and the Electromagnetic Biosphere of human potential. She looks forward to connecting with you to LightenUp together! Sign up for a Free Intuitive Consultation via her website at:

www.lightenup.lol

CHAPTER 23

SELF-LOVE TO SURRENDER

A FEMININE PATH TO EMPOWERMENT

Nicole Jackson, Energy Healing Practitioner,
Womb Wellness Coach, LMT

HOW IT BEGAN

"I think we need some space," were the hurtful words he uttered on that late spring evening. "What do you mean space," I exclaimed? My racing heart now seemed to halt completely; my stomach flipped then reshaped into knots. I could feel the nausea setting in. I could barely breathe. It was as if someone had kicked me in the gut and knocked the wind out of me. I couldn't even remember what we were arguing about. Time stood still. It was surreal. *How could this be happening right now?*" I thought. Trying to hold back the tears was futile. He broke my heart.

Two weeks prior, my boyfriend and I placed everything we needed into a couple of suitcases each, sold most of our belongings, and evacuated our apartment. We had a lofty vision and were delighted to be on our way to Costa Rica to create a new reality. I was 26 at the time, an optimistic, adventurous soul with a strong desire for freedom. This trip would be our escape from a monotonous life. By now, we'd accumulated five years together.

We'd met in college shortly after I turned 21 and had been inseparable since then. Sure, we had our issues as most couples do, but we were in love, or so I thought. I'd soon discover that I was the one in love, not him.

I'd rehearsed it in my mind, romantic strolls at sunset, lots of passionate lovemaking, starting a family, while blissfully living. As time grew closer to our departure, this was all I could think about. What a dream! However, my dream transformed into a nightmare with those upsetting words. Dark clouds rolled in, and a tropical storm emerged within our relationship that would forever change my life.

I moseyed around with a dismal disposition for days. As days became weeks, I internalized what had transpired and even blamed myself for the breakup. My self-confidence plummeted. *Was I not beautiful enough? Not good enough? What did I do wrong?* My mind swirled with unanswered questions. Finally, I came up with my conclusions, none of which empowered me. I was the problem.

Although we were cordial with one another, there was zero intimacy. My grief was apparent. There were days that I barely ate, and in just a few weeks, I went from a size eight to a four. I'd sacrificed six years of my young adult life hoping this relationship would work, and yet it failed. Being honest with myself, I could admit he was all wrong for me. However, fearful of being alone, I ignored my intuitive nudges. In retrospect, I could see it was a classic narcissist/empath relationship. I wanted so desperately to be loved. He needed the attention, devotion, and ultimately the control I'd offer up in return. Yet, I disregarded my internal compass. I was blinded by my hunger for true love and connection.

Now, here I was, living in a foreign country, with a man who'd deserted me. I had no income, no support, and no plan. Damn!

Talk about being stressed out! My response was visceral. My shoulders were like giant boulders attached to my neck. My once brilliant smile gave way to a stoic grin at best, and my hair had even started to fall out. I was a hot mess. And I was freaking furious. Furious at him for abandoning me when I needed him the most, but mostly at myself for giving up my entire life and making poor choices. Even amid all this inner turmoil, I projected a sense of calm. It was as if something inside of me realized that I would get through this. *This too shall pass,* echoed inside my mind. This mantra was a beacon of light in the dark cave of my mind.

Drifting around, repressing my emotions, pretending that I was okay when I wasn't, I lived a state of functional depression. I was aware that my life needed to shift desperately. I knew I needed to begin the journey of forgiving and loving myself, but I didn't know how to. What I did know was that I was living in a tropical paradise and not allowing myself to experience the totality of its beauty. Nature, however, would soon become my closest friend and my pathway to healing.

We found ourselves living on the Caribbean side of the country in a small cottage not very far from the Costa Rica-Panama border. It was a sunny, balmy 80 degrees on most days, and the gentle breeze coming from the ocean seemed to create just the perfect balance. The aroma of ripening fruits, such as mangos, bananas, and guavas, permeated the air. They tasted as divine as they smelled.

A few days a week, there was a local gentleman beaming of life who'd often bring us fresh coconuts. His infectious smile and positive energy were a remedy for my soul. You knew he was coming because he sang joyfully everywhere he went. Life here was simple. *The Pura Vida,* a phrase often used by the locals, translating into pure life. In my observation, people didn't own many material things, yet they were genuinely happy. Happiness is an inside job. It's not about what you possess; it's about who you are being and what you are choosing in the present moment. One of the many lessons I'd come to learn from this journey.

Our house was a brief four-minute walk to the ocean. The soothing sounds of the waves crashing on the shore were hypnotic. It was like being summoned by a pied piper; I began to find my way to the water daily.

Growing up in a small beach town on the Gulf Coast of Florida, I had a natural affinity for the ocean. Being close to the water became my saving grace. I grounded myself in the ivory sand while watching the white cranes soar over the horizon. The blazing sun anointed my golden-brown skin, its beaming rays giving me new life. The environment was medicinal.

Just being near the saltwater was purifying me in ways I could not yet understand. My breathing synced with the sounds of the ocean, my body effortlessly relaxed, and my mood lifted. The beach provided a peaceful escape from an inner world of emotional chaos. In the healing presence of the sea, my mind became tranquil enough to hear Spirit. Sidenote: When I speak of Spirit, I'm referring to the Divine presence that permeates all things. I'm also talking about spirit guides, ancestors, and higher beings. At the time, I had no concept of meditation. Yet, every trip to the beach proved to be a blissful meditational experience that brought me home to my true self. Entranced by the waves, I began to tune out the negative thoughts prevalent in my mind and tune in to a more peaceful zone.

One day, while lying near the water, I heard a voice so clearly as if someone behind me whispered in my ear *You are the love you have been searching for.* What profound wisdom! It's as if someone had just flipped the proverbial light switch, enlightening my soul. Those words shifted everything for me. It was at this moment that my path to empowerment began. It was here, at the ocean, that I would learn the power of surrender.

After about four weeks of holding onto the grief, anger, and frustration I was desperately trying to avoid, a divine intervention occurred. The energy of the ocean summoned me towards her. It seemed as if she could sense all the dead weight I was carrying and wanted to assist me in freeing up my energy. The pull was intense, like a strong magnet drawing me into its field. I knew something magical was about to happen that day. I could feel it in my belly. Instead of questioning my sanity, I trusted the process. As I slowly walked into the water, the tears began streaming; the cleansing effects of the ocean were already working its mojo. Channeling the ocean's voice, I then heard, *Are you ready to let the weight go? Give it all to me so that you may be free.* At that moment, I proclaimed to the Universe, "I am ready to let it all go. I surrender it to you." I then held my breath, lay backward, and fully submerged myself in the revitalizing waters of the sea.

A baptism occurred. I freed myself from the heaviness weighing on my heart, the shame, the guilt, the resentment, the stories of abandonment, even the lies I adopted around unworthiness and not being enough. Although my eyes were closed, I could vividly see myself as an energy being. I witnessed a dull, greyish cloud lifting away from my body and dissolving in the ocean. Instantly my energy field was bright and vibrant. I could feel the electrifying yet soothing presence of what I perceived as love all around me. My heart radiated, and I melted into the waves allowing myself to float for what seemed like hours, although I'm sure it was only 15 minutes at best. I'd experienced oneness. I surrendered to the ocean that day; I was a new woman. My cheeks and lips gave way to the biggest smile I'd had in weeks. *Today was a new beginning, a rebirth.*

THE TURNING POINT

Shortly after, I returned home to Florida to reset my life. I'd entered a newfound place of self-discovery. *Who was I now, not being in a relationship that I had poured so much of myself into? What type of work would I do? What was my purpose?* I didn't have the answer to these questions, yet I knew there was more destined for me than I was allowing in.

A synchronistic sum of occurrences found me in a local bookstore the following year. Life gifts us with those pivotal events, where things are never quite the same after going through them. On this late autumn day in 2006, I'd experience one of those such incidents. Reading was a long-held passion, so I decided to peruse the bookstore close to the mall and enjoy a great cup of chai while there. Before heading over to the café, I took a casual stroll around the store. While approaching a particular aisle, a strange phenomenon occurred within my body. A warm, tingly sensation vibrated from my crown down through my spine. Every sense seemed to heighten. A gentle force bubbled within my being, and it was guiding me towards a particular shelf. Though a bit startling, it was a familiar sensation. My encounter with the ocean flashed across my mental screen; this was no coincidence. Later I'd come to understand this phenomenon as clairsentience, one of my spiritual gifts.

Skimming the titles, I noticed the shelf contained books centered around wellness, vitality, and holistic health. *Right up my alley,* so I thought. Then, suddenly, I noticed a book that seemed to have a faint, shimmering halo. I blinked my eyes a few times to ensure I wasn't seeing things. Surely this book isn't glowing, I thought, but there it was pulsating and emanating a lifeforce of its own. Certainly, this was a sign. When I picked it up, my brow raised. *What is Reiki? Why did this seem so intriguing? Why was Spirit guiding me towards this book?* I sat down in awe, glancing through the beautifully illustrated pages sipping my chai. The concept of energy healing was new and fascinating. It revealed a whole new world. The content of this book forever changed my life. I quickly began implementing the self-healing practices demonstrated inside with sheer excitement and wonder.

I took a deep dive into my spiritual work. I knew to be entirely free; I would have to find it in my heart to forgive those who hurt and betrayed me, including myself. Spirit equipped me with the proper healing tools, and I did the work. I resolved to nurture my inner child. I cradled myself and rocked myself tenderly as I cried rivers of tears. I was releasing energies, silently holding my heart and womb hostage. In reflecting, I had a lot of those ugly cries. You know the ones I'm talking about. I learned first-hand that healing is not all love and light; it can be messy, unpleasant, and cathartic. What's important is, learning to show ourselves some grace and refraining from self-judgment as we move through our transformational process.

SELF- LOVE

My heart chakra expanded like a lotus flower rising out of the mud into beautiful bloom. I was able to hold more compassion for myself and others. Doing the releasing work, I embarked on a journey of self-love. First, I forgave myself for not loving myself. I realized that no one could provide me the love I wasn't willing to give to myself. Spirit revealed that self-love was essential to step fully into my divine purpose.

How can you love yourself more? This question was one that I'd come to ask myself often along my journey. Sometimes the answer was as simple as nourishing me with nutritious foods; other times, it was giving up numb-inducing vices I'd come to lean on. One of my favorite self-love rituals was spending time in nature. Majestic rays of sunlight, coupled with the warm embrace of a giant tree, served as potent remedies to renew my energy.

Presently, nature is still my beloved healing sanctuary. The truth is self-love comes in a myriad of forms. It can be prioritizing your peace over the need to please others. It can be releasing yourself from relationships or situations that don't align with you. Self-love often requires you to put yourself first. Something that many women struggle with, including me. I'd come to realize there are infinite ways to love oneself, and we get to choose what that looks like for us.

We often express self-love as self-care. As a woman who worked two jobs and was always on the go, I rarely set aside time for self-care. I watched my grandmother overwork herself into an early grave, and I refused for this to be my story. I knew I'd come to break these unhealthy generational cycles. So, I became super intentional at self-care. I learned to meditate and started taking a few weekly yoga classes. One positive shift often inspires another. It wasn't long before I changed my diet, eating primarily whole, plant-based foods.

I prioritized my well-being. Within a few months, my body felt and looked incredible. My mind was sharp and clear. The more love I poured into myself, the more radiant I became. The glow-up was real! The more dedicated I became to nurturing myself, the more I softened and embraced my femininity. Goddess energy slowly revealed itself within me. Through the power of self-acceptance, grace, and surrender, I'd finally come to experience the love within myself I so desperately sought from others. I was choosing to fall deeply in love with myself.

WOMB HEALING AND THE FEMININE PATH

Over the next ten years, my walk with Spirit introduced me to various holistic healing modalities. Each one offered a catalyst for my continuous transformation in its unique way. If I had to say what helped me step into my divine feminine energy the most, it'd be womb work.

Sister, did you know that your womb is the seat of your creative power? The most sacred part of your being? I sure didn't. At best, I saw my womb as a source of pleasure, but mostly a source of pain due to the unbearable cramps I experienced monthly during my period. Unearthing the divine nature of my womb was another pivotal moment for me.

I dove deeper into womb healing because I wanted to clear residual sexual trauma stored deep inside my DNA. The cycle would end with me. I imagined this was the source of the pain that'd become such a regular part of my existence. Instead, I'd come to find that our periods don't have to be painful. That insight alone created a shift.

In the spring of 2013, I found myself at a healer's retreat in North Carolina. It was there that I'd meet the woman who introduced me to yoni steaming. Imagine sitting over a wooden box with a hole carved in the center. Underneath lies a pot that contains a concoction of freshly prepared medicinal herbs specifically chosen to address your needs. Warm steam arises from the herbs, permeating and detoxifying your sexual organs for reproductive wellbeing.

Talk about a fantastic discovery! As I began implementing this into my self-love regimen, my cramping drastically reduced, and my periods were much lighter. I even experienced better orgasms. I was a believer! Not only did I feel more empowered in my feminine energy, but I felt at home in my body. After dealing with body shame for most of my life, this was a significant win. My womb and I had healing conversations. I listened to her guidance. A few months afterward, I decided to train with that same woman to become a certified yoni steam practitioner. I love that I get to help women reconnect with their wombs and awaken to their healing potential. **Your healing is my healing. Collectively, our healing is the world's healing. We are one.**

So many of us have been operating more from our masculine energy for far too long. Please don't assume that it's our fault; an imbalanced patriarchal society has long suppressed the power of the divine feminine. However, a planetary shift is occurring, and the new world is being birthed. Feminine energy rises. No longer will she be silenced. She invites you to surrender my sister. Surrender to your spiritual gifts. Surrender to the love that is you! She calls for you to be free, to take control of your destiny, to surrender to all that you came here to be.

Great power lies within your femininity.

Nicole Jackson is the owner of Healthy Soul Wellness LLC. She has been practicing healing arts for over ten years. She is a Master Energy Healer, Certified Health Coach, a Womb Wellness Practitioner, and Massage Therapist. Nicole began her path as a healer by studying Reiki and becoming a Reiki Master in 2007. A few years later, she discovered the energy modality Pranic Healing while attending a Qigong retreat with her mentor Wayne Chandler and later channeled her unique, intuitive style of healing work.

Noticing that food and lifestyle often came up during healing sessions with her clients, Nicole decided to become a Certified Health Coach to assist them better. Therefore, she integrates her knowledge of energy work, nutrition, mindfulness, and self-care into her healing practice.

With a newfound passion for womb healing, Nicole studied with the Yoni Steam Institute in 2013. Her dive into the feminine arts would take her on a six-week sojourn to Thailand to learn Tao Tantric Arts with Minke De Vos and Shashi Solluna. As a result, she became a Sacred Femininity Facilitator and a Certified Healing Love Instructor through Universal Healing Tao (UHT). In 2021, she became a Certified Yin Yoga Teacher with the Body-Mind-Soul Centre. She desires to help set women free from the energetic bondage that holds their joy, creativity, and pleasure hostage. Instead, her mission is to empower her clients to live healthy, sexy, abundant, and blissful lives.

Nicole teaches Qigong and yoga classes and conducts workshops on self-care, womb healing, and sacred femininity. She has facilitated numerous retreats both domestically and internationally. In addition, she has taught classes for corporate organizations, schools, and government agencies. Ultimately, Nicole aims to raise the collective consciousness by helping women step powerfully into their femininity.

To learn more, visit Heathysoulwellness.com.

CHAPTER 24

MAGICAL MOMENTS IN THE MUNDANE

SEIZING EVERY OPPORTUNITY TO GROW

Ashley Hoobler, Spiritual Awakening Coach

"Wait, where is my potato salad? Is everything else in the bag? Yup. It's there." I said out loud to myself that November evening.

I had ordered food for delivery, and it had just arrived. As I pulled out the contents, I noticed I was missing my side dish yet somehow managed to still get the dessert I had ordered. For some reason, this struck me as odd.

I found myself thinking, *of course, they can never get it right! They always forget something. I never manage to get everything that I order.*

I sat on my couch, pondering this for a while. I knew that our experience was a direct manifestation of our internal state. We are surrounded by little clues each day that try to nudge us into paying attention. However, they often go unnoticed. The energy builds and builds, and those nudges get bigger and bigger in our life until they are suddenly a tidal wave crashing upon us and disrupting our daily life. So, I was curious. *What did the missing potato salad mean? Where was I misaligned?* After years of hard work, undoing conditioning, and healing my old karmic crap, I really did not want to get body-slammed by the universe again. Things had been pretty smooth and easy for me since I had taken such radical action to live fully aligned to my own soul's truth.

It took me a little over a month to figure that one out.

Early January, I was messaging back and forth with my friend, and I found this hilarious and a tad sassy picture that I wanted to share on my business page. I was torn between posting it as it was or censoring it. The picture read, "Not everyone is going to think you're gorgeous, amazing, and magical. They are wrong, though. Dickheads." I laughed at the sassy snap back, but I was still unsure if it was appropriate to post with the curse word.

"No, I think it's fine. Just publish it like that. You don't need to censor it! It's not a big deal. Why do you want to censor it anyways?" my friend said.

"Oh shit." I suddenly exclaimed. "I found my potato salad!"

Caught off guard, she was reasonably confused by my sudden transition in the conversation. I explained, "I figured it out! Remember when I was missing my potato salad back in November?"

"Yeah?"

"Well, here it is! I don't get everything I order, and I don't give all of myself in my business." I said.

"I just realized there's this old part of me from the Army that says professionalism looks a certain way. To be professional, I can't use curse words or act silly. Like I have to be this uptight, always together person. I wasn't being my whole self, so I didn't get the whole order."

Inspired, I quickly typed out a post using that image to explain my sudden revelation. As an added slap to the face, I got to the end of my explanation and realized that the picture, the one that said, "Not everyone is going to think you're gorgeous, amazing, and magical. They're wrong, though. Dickheads." was taunting me. I burst out laughing as I realized what the picture was telling me the whole time—be yourself. You can't please everyone. *Thank you, Spirit. I get it now.*

It's strange; I recognize this. But ever since I started to pay attention to my environment and watch for those little mundane things, I started to see such magic and connections within my life. Even the missing potato salad suddenly became magical.

"I better get an extra side dish now!" I joked to my friend later.

About a week later, I had ordered delivery again after working late. I opened the bag, and sure enough, there were extras. *Thank you, Spirit. I figured it out!*

The universe gives us many opportunities to heal ourselves and tries to speak to us in the smallest moments. The ones often overlooked. That is often where the most serendipitous things occur, though. Nothing is ever by chance when living in this way, and it unleashes such beauty and magnificence into your life.

Many times, these little clues in my life have led me to great revelations. As I noticed my inner compass (emotions) and my inner narratives, I easily found those smaller moments where I was not my authentic self.

Many people in the spiritual world talk about the signs from your guides, angels, and deceased loved ones; however, many don't think to mention the undesirable signs in our life. These are the ones that can have such a profound effect on our lives, should we take notice and adjust.

A couple of weeks after I discovered the hidden meaning behind the missing potato salad, I woke up to a pipe that had burst in the shared bathroom and bedroom wall in my room.

I stepped into the bathroom at 3 a.m. after my daughter woke me up.

"Mommy, there's water all over the floor."

Sighing, I look around, the water has seeped into the bedroom carpet along the wall, and the entire bathroom has a thin coat of water over it. What on earth did I do now? The weather isn't cold enough right now for a pipe to burst! Bleary-eyed, I got dressed, sent my daughter back to her room to get a bit of sleep before she had to go to school, and called the landlord for help.

A few hours later, he arrives. Looking down at the mess that the leak caused after the water was off, he said, "This might take a while to fix. You won't have water until I find the pipe and patch it up. There's no telling where the leak is, though."

Frantic, I ask, "Don't you have blueprints for the house that show where the plumbing is?"

"No. These houses don't come with that. I'll have to open up the wall. The pipes are under the foundation, so I'll have to get a jackhammer and bust up the concrete until I find the spot that is leaking."

At this point, I'm creating doomsday scenarios in my mind. A picture forms in my head of him having torn up the floor in my room all the way down the wall, into the living room, and across to the garage.

I message my friend again, who also reads Akashic records. I need an unbiased reading to figure out what caused this energetically. She checks in for me and comes back, "Yup. There's nothing there. I just get this distinct feeling that it's time for you to move."

In the weeks leading up to the pipe bursting, I had kept having these thoughts pop into my head that I needed to start my house search. My lease was up in June, so I kept brushing it off and not doing anything to get it started again. Two days before the pipe broke, I had received an email from the lender I had initially gone with for a preapproval during the past Summer. I had planned to move in December but the email said they were archiving my request due to no action on the account.

Talking with my friend, I ask, "So all of this, just a sign to start my house hunt?" She laughed. "I know I asked for loud, clear signs that I can easily understand, to help me find the right place at the right price, in the right location—but this is not what I meant by that!"

Sitting down at the computer with the jackhammer in the background as my landlord attempted to locate the problem, I pulled up the lender's site and started to submit the requested paperwork.

The next day I greeted my landlord as he returned to continue with the repairs. He stopped and looked grimly at me and said, "You might consider filing a claim with renters insurance and start thinking about finding another place to stay. This could take, optimistically, two weeks to repair."

At That point, I was overwhelmed, frustrated, and frazzled. I was trying to work out the logistics of relocating with a pet, my daughter, and myself. How I would get her to and from school? We usually walked the two blocks. How I would keep seeing clients? What all I would need to take with me for that? These questions along with all of the other details that would go into moving. I was resisting it. I did not want to do that unless absolutely necessary.

Around noon I got a phone call from the lender to congratulate me on my process of buying my first home. They gave me the information I needed and set me up with a networked realtor familiar with the VA loan process and military and veterans benefits. *Finally, something is going my way today!* I busied myself searching for properties and trying to narrow down a location, thinking Spirit would point me to where in the world I should relocate. Still, all I got was silence and no intuitive pulls to anywhere in particular. I started researching myself and creating a list. An hour after getting off the phone with the lender with the good news, my landlord came out to update me.

"The good news is, I found the leak. Can you watch the pipes while I test the water?"

"Sure."

He ran back inside after turning off the water in the street again.

"Did you see it?"

"Yes. It's right there." I point to where the water was spraying out of the pipe.

"That's what I thought! Alright, let me get it patched up, and you can have water again by tonight."

As I made progress on my house hunting, the timeline for repairs began to speed up quickly. By the end of the fourth full day of the debacle, my wall was sealed back up, the carpet was back down, and all that was left to do was to bring all of the items pulled out of the room and bathroom back in and reorganize it. It was like magic. Each small step I took in my house hunt, a big step in fixing the pipe was made. The optimistic two weeks turned into four days, with only 1.5 days without water and a night out of my room.

I look back now, amazed at the synchronicity of it all—the magic in the mundane things. The adverse experiences propelled me forward to grow and live more deeply into my authentic self. I can't help but find myself in awe.

Our authenticity and alignment in life are found in the small details. We choose to stay silent or put on a mask and portray ourselves one way to fit in better. It's so ingrained in our unconscious minds that we don't notice it. It isn't this big event or personality trait we possess most of the time. It's those tiny choices we make each and every day. Noticing those even tinier experiences in our day-to-day gives us the chance to find every opportunity to grow. Personally, and spiritually.

As a Spiritual Awakening Coach, my main focus is working with clients to help them undo their karmic patterns causing the upheaval and adversity in their lives. The more karmic blocks are undone, the easier things become.

As our awareness and alignment increase, the opportunities become more subtle and mundane. If they are left unanswered, the pressure builds— a pipe burst, a tire pops, a wrong order delivered, a package missing, etc. Those frustrating inconveniences, big or small, are all opportunities to grow.

If I have learned anything, it is to find magic within the mundane and seek every opportunity to grow. Those little snags in your day are whispers and warnings from the universe to help guide you the right way. Listen to them, and you too can find the magic in each and every day.

 **Ashley Hoobler** is an Army veteran, single mother, and spiritual leader. Ashley spent 13 years in the Army, which helped her cultivate her leadership, mentorship, and communication skills through her experiences in working with people from all walks of life. In 2020 Ashley opened her spiritual business, Seeking Divine Serendipity, which was created to assist spiritual seekers in healing and transforming their lives, no longer living through struggle after struggle. Ashley focuses most of her work on newly awakened souls who have had their lives turned upside down upon their awakening, who crave a life of stability, peace, and fulfillment. Ashley blends the magic of the Akashic Records, NLP, Coaching, and psychology to help clients break free from old habits and create a new life for themselves.

Ashley has completed six levels of training on the Akashic Records through the Soul Realignment modality and the initial and mastery certifications through Soul Success Unleashed, which teaches aura and clairvoyant readings and energy healing and energy management tools. Ashley has also been certified as a life coach, evolved neurolinguistic programming practitioner, and quantum timeline healing practitioner through Avalon Empowerment. If you want to check out the post Ashley mentions in her story; you can find it here:

https://www.facebook.com/SeekingDivineSerendipity/posts/494696855705257

To learn more about Ashley and her programs, go to www.seekingdivineserendipity.com or email ashley@seekingdivineserendipity.com.

CHAPTER 25

DISMANTLING A TRAUMA AND VICTIM MENTALITY

FINDING COURAGE AND RECLAIMING YOUR POWER.

Bruja Carrie Liz Ramos

We cannot become what we want to be
by remaining what we are.

~Max Depree

The journey of healing is like a revolving door. Some days we easily pass through emotions and unresolved traumas, feeling relieved that it was a breeze to get through. Then on other days, we get stuck, banging on the glass door that refuses to budge even just a little bit. This is the stuck that makes sweat slowly start to trickle down your back; a whirlwind of emotions starts to kick in. This is a test of our character. On those days when you get stuck on a particular emotion or memory, I hope you bravely face it head-on.

It's not easy to share a part of my truth. It's terrifying. A part of me relives it all over again, and a part of me is in awe of my own growth. A hard pill

I've had to swallow is that sometimes those meant to love, protect, and guide you are the very ones to hurt you the most. At least this was the case for me growing up.

From a very early age, I was in fight or flight mode. It's exhausting, but something I became accustomed to. I was given no choice. My childhood was filled with some happy memories, but also ones tainted with witnessing domestic violence, verbal and emotional abuse, lies, and adultery. There was a definite lack of love. My father left when I was eight, and my mother quickly remarried to someone worse. A void was left inside of me from a very young age. At the time, I couldn't process it all. *Why me? What did I do wrong?*

Let me take you back to thirteen-year-old Carrie. This is her story.

As a night owl, the peaceful silence of everyone else being asleep was comforting. Being wide awake made me feel like the world was mine—no one to yell, pick at or judge me. This was my favorite time of day. I used to take showers late at night, especially if I was up binging on the latest Harry Potter book or catching up on homework.

One evening I was in the bathroom, doing shower things, humming along to a song in my head, shaving my legs when suddenly a loud crash reverberated against the walls. The familiar violent tones of my mom and stepdad yelling filled the silence. I froze, trying to hear what was going on. It sounded ugly, whatever it was. My mom pounded on the wooden pocket door of the bathroom and told me, "Get out!"

Water dripping everywhere, I hastily dried off and put on my clothes. Here we go again; somehow, I was in trouble. *What did I do now?!* I remember my clothes sticking to me and how confused I felt as my mother said, "Your stepdad was watching you shower." A peeping Tom. She broke a glass bottle over his head when she caught him. He was peeping with a mirror under the door.

My whole world crashed around me. I started to dry heave, but nothing would come out. The argument carried on for what felt like an eternity. I remember thinking: *It's your fault for showering so late, stupid. Ew, he's supposed to be my stepdad. This is so gross. Why me?!*

"Go to sleep; we'll talk about it in the morning," my mother said. That night I cried myself to sleep, hoping to drown in my tears. I felt so violated and empty. I barely had a girlish figure. My mom would say my body was very boxy, like a boy. I hadn't even started my period; I was barely a woman, and yet here we were.

The next day, I didn't get out of bed. I remained under the safety of a heavy, baby blue blanket. He quietly knocked on my door and let himself in. He whispered, pleading, "It didn't happen. Your mom made it up. I would never do that do you. I love you guys."

He walked out and quietly shut my bedroom door. That moment broke me. I knew what they would do—sweep it under the rug and pretend like everything was okay. But I wasn't. A silent raging little girl sat inside me, begging to be loved, begging for anyone to stand up for me, begging for clarity and for someone to say, "This is wrong!" This is how I lived until I was able to move out.

It took quite a bit of time to break free from the toxic cycles and relationships that did not serve me. I made many mistakes along the way to get to this version of who I am today. For years, paranoia followed me going into any bathroom. I had a routine of locking the door and making sure it was locked. I scanned the room to look for any cracks or possible ways for someone to watch me. I stared at the bottom of the door for a bit as I talked myself down to a calmer place. I'm proud to say I no longer carry this fear with me.

It's time for this story to be shared. I'm no longer that thirteen-year-old girl with no voice. I now speak up and stand up for those who share similar experiences. Past generations need to address these traumas for them to be healed. I find that the victims are silenced and the abusers protected in certain communities. It was never my fault, and I didn't deserve any of what I went through. I'm now able to stand firm in my own version of courage. The courage to say no. The courage to speak my own truth.

Forgiveness is a funny word. What does it actually mean, and how is the best way to go about this? As weird a concept as it was for me to understand, it was the very word I needed to embrace to heal and hold space to release the pent-up anger. My need for inner peace was stronger than the desire to hold onto that anger. Anger can swim through your veins like poison and sour everything it comes into contact with. While I will never forget my experiences, I release the pain by forgiving my family. Through my own healing journey, I recognized their need for healing too. A major part of my awakening to my spiritual path started with awareness and self-reflection. It was painful to replay those memories, but also necessary. The need for validation was strong. Speaking your truth is not an easy task. I've had to cut ties and end relationships, the most difficult being with my family. The mentality of my acts of rebellion or insecurities being their fault was what I had to outgrow.

I placed firm boundaries so I could experience peace. I cut out my stepdad from my life in my early 20s. I remember cussing him out and calling him a pervert. It felt good to acknowledge my pain and call him out. To this day, his family has no idea of his behavior, and as an adult, I do not need him to pretend to be a father figure. My mother has since been in and out of my life. I love my mother. However, her lack of accountability has me keeping my distance. My mother refuses to heal or change. She never left him; she never chose to protect me. Many times she would say, "Don't wear those shorts," or "That's what you want to wear?!" It's like she blamed me for his behavior as if I competed with her somehow. I am half of her. I saw the lack of self-worth and self-love she had transferred into how she loved me. Codependency and narcissistic traits require professional therapy. They knew what they were doing and chose not to care about the consequences. Reflecting on all of this now, as I mother myself, I couldn't fathom doing the same to my own girls. Sometimes distance is self-care.

We can choose to relearn what love is. We can choose to reparent ourselves. We can choose to be different. It's possible to find family among peers who've gone through similar experiences and are working on themselves. We can choose to be accountable and hold space for our own healing. This will be a continuous process, but the reward of breaking free of these toxic cycles is worth it. Reclaiming your power has everything to do with your mindset moving forward. Moving forward, I choose peace; I choose love; I choose myself. For those struggling through this, I wish for you to have the strength to stand up for yourself and keep going.

Dance and music have been my greatest form of therapy, as well as journaling. I've found joy in getting lost in nature and embracing whatever adventures nature sends my way. There is power in saltwater, so I make the drive to the beach as often as possible. There is something about watching the sunrise and listening to the seagulls calling and waves crashing. Nature has a beautiful way of giving us music to heal. People often choose to find their escape with alcohol, drugs, or promiscuity. I've been down that path and recognized it wasn't what was best for me. I haven't always been the best person. I've hurt others, lied, cheated, and made many mistakes. It takes a lot to admit past failures, but even more to ask for help and see the changes that need to happen. This is not easy by any means, but I wouldn't go back. Each day I strive to be a better version of my yesterday. Laughter is some of the greatest medicine we have. Learning to rest and include daily self-care is a must-have to live as consciously awakened souls.

In the moments that break and bury us, there's a choice. We can be reborn from the very pain that hurt us, transmuting that energy to lift us up rather than tear us down. This is your time; give yourself permission to take charge of your life. Reclaim your power! Allow yourself to release the shame, confusion, doubt, and fear. There is divine purpose to every experience we have. How will you choose to lead?

Try this as medicine from me to you whenever you're feeling overwhelmed.

Xoxo - C

SPIRITUAL BATH FOR CLEANSING YOUR ENERGY:

I prefer to do this simple bath before going to bed. There are many traditions or ways to go about it. Follow what you feel called to do! The most important part is your why; intention is everything.

INGREDIENTS:

- Moon water
- Sea salt, pink Himalayan salt
- Fresh or dried herbs: eucalyptus, peppermint, basil (epazote, rue, or hyssop for my advanced herb lovers)

INSTRUCTIONS:

- Boil water, add herbs and salts to hot water. Cut off heat. Allow them to steep for 10-13 minutes. Bring herb water to the bathroom. I like to add bay rum cologne, Florida water cologne, or holy water once it's cooled down. Say a prayer from the heart to bless the mixture.

- Take a shower. Cleaning your physical body from head to toe is a necessary first step.

- Shut off the shower. Pour herb and salt mixture from the shoulders down. Air dry.

- You can mix spiritual oils with your favorite fragrance-free lotion to moisturize your body before getting dressed.

- Repeat. I like to do this bath for three, seven, or nine nights in a row, depending on how the energy feels.

- Bonus: Make sure to properly thank the herbs for their blessing of healing and bury them outside.

Carrie is a Puerto Rican Bruja, Espiritista, Tarot reader, and energy healer.

Originally from Connecticut, she has traveled all over the country and now lives in Florida with her two little brujitas and two cats.

Connecting back to her native roots, Carrie discovered Santeras, espiritistas, muerteros, and a few curanderos in her family lineage. This knowledge was a catalyst into her own spirituality. She has been reading tarot since she was a teenager and now professionally for six years.

As an intuitive psychic healer and witch, she loves to help others navigate their spiritual journey and discover their life purpose.

She focuses primarily on self-love and healing—the relationship we have with ourselves is a major influence on what we bring into our lives. Bruja Carrie Liz finds it gratifying to help others find their way and nurture healthy, loving relationships.

Carrie has aspirations of opening up her own local Botanica and spiritual shop. Speaking your dreams into existence is a firm belief of hers. For now, she virtually offers spiritual mentoring, tarot readings, energy healing, and various candle services.

To reach out or book a service, visit www.TheBrujaChronicles.com

Follow Bruja Carrie Liz on Instagram, Youtube, Twitter, and Tiktok.

EPILOGUE

I don't typically dream, but when I do, I remember each and every detail. This morning I experienced a dream that will remain with me for some time. Certainly, an impactful message from my guides, as I set out to write this final bit for *Sister Armor*. This message isn't just for me; it's for all of us, so it's important I share.

I sat on an ottoman, looking up at a felicitous bird who was in a birdcage. We made eye contact. I looked slightly closer only to realize the bird had gotten too big for its cage. I said, "Oh, look at you, you're awfully big for this cage. I suppose it's time for a new one." The bird and I locked eyes again. A floating moment of stillness. I asked, "Do you want a bigger birdcage, or would you prefer to be set free?" I looked down at my hands, and when I looked back to the bird, it was gone—the cage, the bird, all of it, gone. The bird chose to be set free, along with the self-imposed cage.

I can't help but think how this very question is being posed to all of us. Will you simply expand the cage you're in, or will you release yourself and be free? Think of one thing in your life that holds you back and sabotages your success and joy. It may feel like a dark prison, but you already have the key. Fill yourself up with love and self-honoring and see yourself taking your next steps to freedom.

The moment you picked up *Sister Armor, Healing in Community* and engaged in these stories, you began your unique journey. It's safe to recognize your efforts. You've been traveling on your own while at the same time joining together with the collective energies of others committed to healing. You may not see it or realize it at this point, but the unseen and physical worlds are woven together. Worlds interconnected and unlimited are here to support as we navigate and respond to the calls of our hearts.

This book has come forth to assist you in the greatest time of healing. Benevolent beings, guides, and loved ones are preparing you now for greatness. They're bestowing blessings upon you, guiding you to infinite paths, outlying and illuminating purpose-filled paths you haven't been able to see prior to today. Allow yourself, more and more, to be within this sacred energetic space. Reside here to allow the flow of intelligent downloads to pour through your divine channel. In this timeline lies great realization and production for you. There will be a lot of births at this time and continuing through the duration of your life.

You'll find yourself having to do more than read books, take classes, and attend plant medicine ceremonies. It'll be important to find ways to evolve your everyday life so that you're developing your inner life and weaving spiritual practices into your daily life. You'll ultimately find yourself embodying this intention. There will be no denying the guidance in living a life filled with a higher purpose.

Tune in to the energy that's all around you. Being familiar with energetic patterns arms you in using your discernment. This means the energy of others, places, plant life, the animal kingdom, and that of your own. Attuning to energy is a big part of what healing is. The more we welcome stillness for internal connection, the more we open active conversation. This will aid you in seeing beyond the physical facade being presented. It's an innate tool that supplies you with sight; a scope to identify what is or isn't in alignment with you.

Build a rapport with this living intelligence. You'll quickly come to know what feels good to you and what doesn't. If an energetic connection makes you question its intention, it's likely not energy you'd wish to work with. You get to say what is right for you and what is not. During connections, we open ourselves up and act as a conduit to the spirit world. So it'll be important for you to honor your innate cues and senses. Trust yourself. There are endless possibilities to the information spirit can pass along through you. Spirit is intelligent, always bringing you exactly what you need, and they will present it in a way that's an undeniable message for you. Having that kind of interaction with the spirit world is very special. This is sacred work. It allows you to be exactly what you are meant to be— an intermediary between this world and the next.

There is a highly organized order to the universe. We come here to walk through this life to learn lessons, accomplish things, grow. There are beings in the spirit world helping us to do that, and it's not helpful to them or us when we believe otherwise. In society, we've been operating under dense energetic emotions: jealousy, comparison, and insecurity. These types of energetic forms keep us from connecting to truth and living in truth. Comparison is the thief of joy, and it blocks our individual infinite flow.

Never settle for anything less than aligned relationships on your spiritual journey. This includes teachers and healers, communities, churches, and circles. If someone ever attempts to dictate or control how you honor your connection with Divine, they are not for you. This won't always be obvious. Though as you learn what it is you need, directed by only you, then boundary setting and saying "no" becomes easy. Listen intently. Setting boundaries is a command of self-love.

Those who've gone before you have shined a light into the darkness and revealed the spirit world to those who needed to see it most. Choose to be a keeper of the light. Transmute the energy behind your thoughts and words: you are feeding yourself and the world with light. Remember, what you feed grows. What you give energy to, you give life to. You are encouraged to ground and root yourself in your heart. Know that your ancestors are working on your behalf. They love you, and they impart gifts and strengths to you so you may thrive and be successful and healthy.

I hope the stories of *Sister Armor* anchor moments of sacred union in the cells of your body that lead you to re-join with sacred aspects of Self, allowing you to begin a new journey within your human experience. I hope it allows you to let go of many old hurts and concepts and to be able to appreciate a deeper level of love for yourself. I hope that, in turn, allows you to extend compassion toward yourself and also extend that compassion and love to others. I hope this helps you gain a greater understanding of the journey, and through that clarity, supports engagement with your divine self, deepening that connection. Each time you sit in the power of Spirit, these moments of connection transform you to greater self-love.

Trust who you are. You are more than an ego; you are Spirit; you are a being of divine light. You were created from a place of unconditional love. Hold the vision of the world in which you wish to live. Living a spiritual life lifts the mental horizons and lets in the heavens. One may compare this to releasing from their self-imposed birdcage. Don't forget in the darkness what you learned in the light.

Learn to let go of distractions from life and fully engage in your spiritual work. It's also important to hold a strong focus and stay true to your intention while surrendering the outcome. As you manifest desired outcomes, surrender! We're conditioned to demand instant gratification. However, we must first be in a place of allowance and flow to create a new reality. One piece of straw at a time is what builds the bird's nest. Lean into your heart, intuitive creativity, and intentions to create a life filled with meaning and passion. All of this is energy.

So it is with great love and deep gratitude that I move forward. Know that I hold the platform of this completion journey for each one of you, and it is my deep wish for you to join me in holding this essential platform for others who will follow. Remember, whenever you experience harmony within, there will be harmony without in the world.

My high love to you,
Tiffany Marie

ACKNOWLEDGMENTS

A heart of gratitude to all of the courageous authors presented in this book. It has been an absolute pleasure getting to know and work with each of you. I am in deep gratitude to you for allowing yourself to go "there." I see you and honor you.

A huge shoutout to Laura, Alex, and the rest of the Brave Healer Productions team! I am grateful for your ability to hold the space necessary for these books!

To my unwavering Armor. Matt, Madison, and Hailey. Your love is the greatest wealth. I love you so very much.

My heart to my parents. I love you so deeply. I give thanks and honor you. The pain and trauma you've endured granted lessons that have saved and healed the new ancestors.

To Paul, Tina, Carla, Tyisha, Laura, Bernadette and Smirah. We have known each other since childhood; what a beautiful gift to dance with you in this life. Thank you for always inspiring and empowering me and the world.

To Ms. Leslie for her brilliance. Thank you for being on-call and excited to help.

To Brittany, "Ginger", for her fierce intuitive creativity. Thank you-you were meant to be a part of this mission.

My devotion and love to the helping spirits for the continual teachings of how to live a life filled with joy and meaning and the teachings of how to help others do the same.

THE RECONNECTIVE WAY HEALING PROGRAM

It feels important that I talk about, and describe to you, the body of work that was channeled through me and that is currently being offered globally.

Read testimonials at www.bodyandsoulconnection.com

The ReConnective Way is the first channeled work I have anchored into this timeline. Much more is scheduled to derive from this work. There is no denying we are in a time of receiving profound healing possibilities. Many healings that have been forgotten and hidden from us are on the rise; we are remembering ancient teachings and wisdom. *The ReConnective Way* is one.

The *ReConnective Way* approach is one of a comprehensive thought-form that unifies a disconnection, which occurs at an originating soul level plane of the human's state of being. This approach reclaims what was separated from the human energy field—resulting in abundant spiritual and vital health.

Within a single-life experience forms needs for the human self, i.e., survival basics, belief, and thought systems and forms, religion, financial (in)securities, relationship exchanges, human illness, disease, etc., are all concepts the soul witnesses and adapts too. Meaning, each time the soul incarnates, it has the foundation (or to say "a manual") of being a human already encoded. Yet, what happens here is the soul adapts so well that it takes on forms or facades that don't necessarily support itself—making human life unnecessarily tumultuous or untimely.

The ReConnective Way illuminates and clears debris, contracts, and particle facades that have acquired themselves as residual from other timely incarnations. While also connecting to channels and portals in direct line with the Divine Soul. With each incarnation, the soul has been encrusted by contracts, belief systems, illness/disease, hereditary conditions, etc., profoundly making it more and more true to factual. Unbeknownst to us, we continue to "drag" these encrusted concepts into our existence. *ReConnective Way* breaks or releases the "crust" and stops these cycles by removing formed facades and re-connecting the energy portals and soul line cords, ultimately illuminating an individual's greatest purpose path.

The most recent evidence continues to impress and convinces us to proceed with excitement and curiosity. A complete representation of this healing will continue to be documented and shared.

To learn more about *ReConnective Way* and to schedule a consultation, visit www.bodyandsoulconnection.com

SISTER ARMOR HEALING RETREAT

The authors of *Sister Armor, Healing in Community* are proud to announce a healing retreat! To learn more and register, visit www.bodyandsoulconnection.com

Unravel only to realize you already are everything you need. Trust in your will and break free. We are meant to live to our highest potential; let's not be imposed by the stories spoken onto us. Make your own story. You are worthy of that much, my dear.

~Tiffany Marie

Made in the USA
Middletown, DE
19 June 2022

67305660R00133